LIVE PASSIONATELY

LIVE PASSIONATELY

The Blueprint to Design

a Life Truly Worth Living

Moustafa Hamwi

PASSIONPRENEUR
PUBLISHING

Publishing information
Publishing, design, and production facilitated by Passionpreneur Publishing,
www.PassionpreneurPublishing.com.

What Global Leaders Are Saying about Moustafa

Moustafa is one of the great 100 Leaders & Coaches of the future.
Dr Marshall Goldsmith
World's #1 Executive Coach

One of the few individuals that truly understands the power of passion and is making a real difference in the world.
John Mattone
World's #1 Authority on Intelligent Leadership

If I can give you one advise: if you lack passion call Moustafa!
Fons Trompenaars
World's Leading Authority on Corporate Culture

Moustafa…Mr. Passion!
Prof. Tony Buzan
Inventor of Mind Mapping
Nobel Peace Prize Nominee

To Mom and Dad

I'm everything I am
because you sacrificed everything you could
in the pursuit of your true passion and purpose:
being the best parents you could be.

Table of Contents

Acknowledgements

I owe a big thank-you to a lot of people who helped this book see light; below, I list only a few, simply because I will need a full book to acknowledge them all.

To my family:

- Bushra and Arwa, my sisters, for being the yin and yang in my life;
- Yousef, my brother, for being as candid as can be;
- Seema, my niece, for being my sounding board throughout this book journey.
- and Diana, my soulmate, for being by my side every step of the way.

To my mentors:

- The late Prof. Tony Buzan, for honouring me with the title "Mr Passion" and the valuable contribution Mind Mapping had on my life;
- Dr Marshall Goldsmith, for believing in me (I would have still been searching for direction without your guidance);

- Brian Tracy, for inspiring a generation to pursue success and personal growth before I even met him and for his insights that greatly contributed to the definition of passion;
- Ron Kaufman, for being genuinely caring and supportive early on in my speaking career;
- and Fons Trompenaars for being as philosophically whimsical as can be and for contributing to the passion definition.

To my business partners:

- Ram and Gautam Ganglani of Right Selection, for being with me on the journey of going from "no-guy" to "passion-guy";
- Natasa and Stuart Denman of Ultimate 48 Hour Author for being part of my publishing business journey;
- and Sohin Lakhani from Embassy Books for pushing me to re read my own book so many times before I published it.

To that gentleman who stopped me and said, "You changed my life!" which triggered me on my journey of helping to make the world a more passionate place.

Finally, to all those who supported me but whom I missed to mention on this page, know that, in my heart, I will always appreciate your support.

INTRO

You Are AWESOME

It's lack of faith that makes people afraid of meeting challenges, and I believed in myself.

—Muhammed Ali

Fellow Passion-Seeker,

Are you looking for an opportunity to bring passion back into your life in a way that will positively impact your career, business, relationships, and lifestyle like never before?

If you are just itching to build the life you're dying to live, you're in the right place. Welcome to *Live Passionately*, the interactive book that will help you *Design a Life Truly Worth Living* through a simple and enjoyable process.

I am honoured to have you here, and I want to start by saying:

YOU ARE AWESOME.

You are so phenomenal for taking action towards pursuing your passion.

I am honoured to serve you because you are committed and dedicated to living the most passionate life possible, and I promise you I will deliver; I will make this worthwhile for you.

For those of you who do not know me yet, I'm Moustafa Hamwi, known globally as The Passionpreneur. I am the founder of Passionpreneur Organization, a social enterprise dedicated to helping passionate entrepreneurs harness passion as a competitive advantage to become thought leaders, build a business around their personal brand, and dominate their market.

I have helped TENS OF THOUSANDS of people who are seeking their purpose; I have seen them move on from being lost, confused, and disoriented about their direction in life, relationships, and lifestyle to waking up every morning and loving every aspect of their life!

Through this book, you have the opportunity to access the world's best-of-class content to help you discover your passion with absolute clarity. You're going to be able to design how you want to live your life on your own terms and have your own passion meditation and visualisation process. That is correct—there is a meditation technique in this programme, and you can already go to www.Moustafa.com/PassionTools and enter the code 7,777,777 to download your bonus pack, which includes the passion meditation, an inspirational posters deck, a guide to turning your passion into a successful business, and access to the Passion Tribe private Facebook Group to download your bonus meditation!

That you are holding this book is the greatest evidence that you are ready to take full ownership of your life and transform it into the greater and grander life it is meant to be, and *Live Passionately* (#LivePassionately) will be your guide to doing so.

It is going to be worth every minute of your time, and it's going to be one of the most practical and transformational, yet enjoyable, books you have ever gone through.

WHY This Book?

Every minute you spend should bring you maximum fulfilment. *Live Passionately* will help you design and live your life with grand success and fun.

After going through this book, you will never search for the meaning of your life again. You will wake up each morning feeling confident about yourself and secure of your place in the world. Decisions will become easy to make because you will know what is truly important to you.

This book will help you transform your life into a more passionate and fulfilling life. Your motivation is going to go through the roof as you get the maximum value of every single minute of your life.

Isn't that how you want to live?

Just know where you are and where you want to get to! Then it's easier to understand how to make it happen and what the bigger picture is in all of this. This book is going to help you get clarity on what makes you tick in life: your true passion, purpose, and calling.

Have you noticed how some people, no matter how successful they are, seem to NEVER be fulfilled? They constantly complain about being drained and lacking joy? They are part of the rat race even though they live in a golden cage!

As you follow the course of *Live Passionately*, you will not only have happiness and joy but also the fulfilment that only comes when you are achieving way more than you ever dreamed you would while still having fun.

Let's Party

If there's one thing that I learned from my previous businesses, it is that you cannot have a party alone. We go through our lives surrounded by people of all kinds. When you go through your passion journey, you will not be alone. You will become part of a Passion Tribe—a power group of Passionpreneurs like you.

These are truly passionate people who are making their money doing what they love while changing the world. They are people on the same journey who understand your struggles and your pain and share their knowledge and their resources. They support and cheer each other on.

These are also people who will hold you accountable on this journey and who will hold your hand and go together with you to inspire the world and live an inspiring life. You are going to build your own Passion Tribe—a network of like-minded people who are on a similar journey.

HOW to Use This Book

This book is intentionally designed to be interactive; the days of a book being nothing but a book are long gone. *Live Passionately* becomes more personalised based on how you interact with it. After all, your passionate life is yours and nobody else's!

You can read this book and work with it at your own pace. After sharing my story and how this book came about, which provides context for what I am about to share and inspiration to hang on when things get tough, the chapters of this book can be grouped into three key sections.

Section A: The Foundation of Going on a Passion Journey

New results require a new mindset, so this section lays the right foundation to discovering and living your life in a passionate way. Chapters 2 and 3 of your journey help clear out the confusion about the pursuit of happiness, clarify the true meaning of passion, and set you up for success.

Section B: Core Passion Chapters

This section covers chapters 4, 5, and 6 of the process, which take you on a deep dive into everything that represents true passion in your heart and mind. Gain clarity on what your findings mean, and more importantly, design a passionate lifestyle that culminates with you writing your Passion Statement.

Section C: Passion Continuity Chapters

This section covers chapters 7 and 8, where you will get to visualise your passionate future and build your Passion Tribe so you can have fun while living your passionate life.

Treat this as a working manual so that you have everything in one place and *Live Passionately* becomes your go-to manual for your life! If you are truly serious about pursuing your passion, you'll want to complete this book because it's going to be a GAME CHANGER for you. As long as you do the exercises, you will get results from every single chapter by itself.

The Deal-Breaker

Before we start, I want to tell you something. There's a deal-breaker. For *Live Passionately* to work, there is a fundamental requirement to believe in yourself.

You Are Never Going To Have A Life Until You Start Believing In Yourself.

— Moustafa Hamwi

People out there are waiting, just waiting, for somebody to believe in them, when all they have to do is believe in themselves. I aim to have you get back in touch with that powerful "inner you" who has been quiet for far too long. And I know that you are ready for it and that you DO believe in yourself; that's why you are here reading this book. So, well done!

I'm honoured to serve you.

I promise you that by the time you are done with this book, you are going to be a powerful passion generator and a crucial part of our Passionpreneur movement—a movement of passionate entrepreneurs who are changing the world and living an amazing life while doing it.

Until then, Live Passionately—a life truly worth living, a life to die for.

Moustafa Hamwi

The Passionpreneur

CHAPTER 1

CAVALLI TO MANALI
One-Way Ticket
out of Dubai

Courage is a love affair with the unknown.

—Osho

Do You Know What Makes You Tick?

Without knowing the answer to this question, you will always feel like something is missing, no matter how successful you are, which is how I felt many years ago when I was running a multi million dollar business in Dubai while living a seemingly successful life.

I was co-founder of a communications firm involved in events, entertainment, and modelling, with 45 full-time employees, a 6,000-square-foot office, and partners who were pretty much ruling the nightlife in town. Our holding group at that time had created the most successful nightlife ventures, one of which was the first global Cavalli Club, a $30 million restaurant-lounge designed by the famous fashion designer Roberto Cavalli.

I will leave it to you to imagine how my lifestyle was!

Although my life looked super successful on the outside, like the stuff you see in movies and rap videos, I was all empty on the inside. Sure enough, I had a nervous breakdown and started waking up every day, dreading going to work—the same business that, at one point in time, was my dream come true!

My business was great, and my lifestyle was enviable, but I wanted more out of life than this golden cage. I kept asking myself, "WHAT AM I DOING WITH MY LIFE?" It became increasingly apparent that having clarity about one's passion and purpose affects one more than just direction; it impacts the quality of life and increases the probability of success!

This question triggered me to start an inner search of true passion, purpose, and meaning.

I spent years and tens of thousands of dollars on courses, books, documentaries, and educational programmes, trying to learn everything related to the topic. Although I spent years on my journey, I never found that one source that did it for me. There were are a lot of either self-proclaimed "best" programmes and books, which never lived up to the promise, or very shallow content that barely scratched the surface without any profound revelations on the matter.

For four long years, from 2008 to 2012, I sought and searched in vain, till one day it hit me that there was no single definitive source on the topic simply because most of them just regurgitated existing material without adding too much thought into how all of it can work together to provide a complete meal rather than nibbles that would soon enough leave me looking for more.

It was no longer okay to wake up every day feeling lost and confused. I realised that without knowing the answer to this all-consuming question, I would continue to feel empty.

The Guru from the Caves

By mid-2012, my search introduced me to vipassana, a meditation technique where we spent 10 days in absolute silence (16 hours a day of silent meditation). You can imagine how such an experience was for a hyperactive person living in the fast lane.

One of my revelations during the meditation was this:

At a certain stage of our spiritual evolution, there is a point where you have to give up who you are to become who you are meant to be.

—Moustafa Hamwi

I was at the stage now where I had to go deeper on my journey inwards before I looked for resources outwards. I remember waking up one day with a jolt of energy and a thought that got stuck in a loop in my head: "I'm going to India."

And so I bought a one-way ticket to India.

I had no clear plan of where in India I was going or even what I would do there. I recall my mother asking me, "What are you going to do in India?" And, with no hesitation, my answer was, "I'm going to get lost." That's all that I knew at the moment.

The story of my journey from Cavalli to Manali is a whole book in itself, but not the purpose of *Live Passionately*. I will, however, share two key incidents that stand out for me and that were pivotal in my life.

The first of them could be described (for lack of a better word) as a coincidence—meeting Swami Yogananda who had been meditating in caves for over 13 years. He had just stepped out of a life of solitude and meditation and started teaching wisdom-seekers in his *ashram* in a small village outside the town of Manali in the Himalayas.

On one of my many deep conversations with him, trying to get an answer about life and the purpose and meaning of everything, he said, playing with his long beard, in an Indian accent,

"Do you know what you are thirsty for? If you do not know what you are thirsty for, you cannot quench your thirst."

His words made me realise that while I had bought this one-way ticket to India seeking an answer, I did not even have the most essential element right: the question!

The Wake-Up Call

I had no clue what I was thirsty for! I realised that the more glamorous my life had become, the emptier I had felt. Most of us, while in the pursuit of happiness, lose sight of our ultimate destination, and get stuck in the rat race for more money. And here, I needed a man who had spent a considerable chunk of his life in caves to jolt me out of that daze.

As my journey continued from one place to the next, across the span of this vast, beautiful landscape that is India, I experienced another coincidence (if you still believe in coincidences). One day, on my way to the meditation centre, I decided to walk into a hospital to get myself checked up. When the results came in, I felt as if my life stopped and everything crumbled and collapsed around me; I was told that I had benign prostate enlargement that was, at that moment, labelled medically as an incurable disease!

Suddenly, nothing mattered any more. When something this serious hits you, life halts for a moment while a dozen questions and a hundred scenarios pop into your head—all at the same time! You ask yourself some serious questions about life (or death).

As I left the hospital, I had a few realisations that were crucial to my journey of healing, the first of them being that the word "disease" contains two syllables—"dis" and "ease"—which means to have a lack of ease within you. This lack of ease causes your organs to develop less than perfect health, thereby leading to what is known as an ailment or a disease. If you pay attention to the way people talk about disease, you'll hear them say "developed" and not caught, like one would "catch" the flu.

The disease first starts in the mind (well, actually they begin in the spiritual space, but this is too deep of a discussion for now). So once you heal your mind and soul, your "dis-ease" goes away.

The second realisation was that I was in India, the motherland of healing!

There are no coincidences; if there was a time and place for me to heal from my "dis-ease," then this was it!

It suddenly seemed that all the years I had invested in studying and researching all matters related to the well-being of mind, body, and soul were geared towards one purpose: to prepare me for dealing with this situation. And so it was. I dedicated all my time and energy towards healing with the help of everything I had access to: Ayurveda, vegan diets, juicing, and all kinds of meditations (including laughter meditation and crying meditation). You name it, and I did it. And as you might have guessed, I eventually healed!*

Live Passionately, however, is not about physical healing and medical miracles.

I am here to talk to you about the self-reflection I had to go through when I faced the reality of a serious "WHAT IF...?"

*I am not a medical doctor. Nor am I giving you medical advice. I am only sharing my experience. I do not, thus, take any responsibility for you choosing to go to or not to go to a doctor for any medical condition you have.

What if this was cancer?

What if I had not discovered my condition early and it had turned into lethal cancer in the future?

What if this did not heal?

What if these were the last days of my life?

If so, DID MY LIFE REALLY MATTER?

I asked myself three specific questions that I urge you to ask yourself:

1. Was I FULLY ENGAGED WITH LIFE or was I just a tourist?

2. Did I live a life that was MEANINGFUL TO ME or did I just comply with people's expectations?

3. Did I leave a LEGACY and IMPACT that I was proud of?

In my case, at that time, the answer to all three questions was a big NO!

I don't know what to tell you...

Imagine you live your life, thinking you are on top of the world—you're ruling, you're the king, you're "it." And then, you realise none of this is worth it. When it's time for you to kick the bucket, you are going to reflect on your life in a totally different manner. Luckily for me, I realised the following:

Time is more valuable than money. You can get more money, but you cannot get more time.

—Jim Rohn

Thus, I ask you to look very carefully into your life and ask if your apparent success is masking the real answers to these questions and stopping you from getting 100% fulfilment out of your life. Are you pursuing outer success at the expense of inner fulfilment?

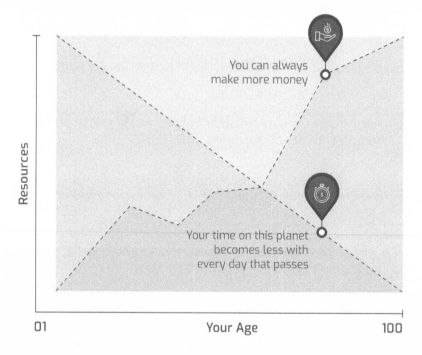

The Answer

A few months after my healing, as I continued my journey across India, I woke up one day with another strong jolt of energy like the one that got me to buy the one-way ticket to India, only this time the voice in my head was saying, "I'm going back to Dubai." And there I was. The journey that started in 2012 ended in 2013, with me buying my ticket back to Dubai.

After my arrival, I had to take on some consulting work to pay the bills, till I figured out how I was going to rebuild my life—the passionate life I aspired to. To keep my fire of passion alive, I made sure I took part in every inspirational event possible. However, one day, I found myself invited to take part in a TEDx-style talk about my journey to India, which was an overwhelming experience, to say the least.

The whole week before the talk I'd get teary-eyed every time I thought about what I was going to do: stand in front of a large group of complete strangers and reveal parts of my life that I had never told anyone about.

However, I used all this emotional charge to energize myself on stage, to put my heart out with no holds barred, to speak with no fear, and it was nothing less than a heartfelt, standing ovation.

A few months after this talk, I was working on the terrace of a hotel in Dubai. One gentleman walked up to me and said, "Hey, are you that speaker guy?"

I said, "Yes."

He said, "You did a talk about your India journey."

I said, "Yes."

He exclaimed, "You changed my life!"

And that was the AHA! moment for me. I suddenly found out what I was thirsty for—being able to change people's lives with my work!

Soon after, self-doubt kicked in; the voice in my head kept saying, "Who do you think you are? This is just a random incident, so just get back to your work." And so it was. I kept at the consulting work that I was doing, and my frustration with life started to increase.

At the same time, more and more of such "You changed my life" incidents started happening in the following months till it became undeniably apparent that this was a sign. It was my calling, and I was not willing to wait till I got into another extreme that required a one-way ticket before I responded. I was not going to let fear take over!

I now wanted to be able to build a legacy around transforming people's lives. And I promise you that, even today, NOTHING comes close to hearing an unsolicited "Thank you for coming into my life."

I was lucky to have found my calling when I was in my mid 30s. This is not such a bad time to reset your life; it surely beats finding it in your 70s or 80s!

Yet I wish I had someone to help guide me on my journey earlier in life; it might have saved me a lot of the loss and confusion I went through. So I decided to be that person for others.

This is not to say that I do not totally appreciate this journey that made me who I am today; however, this is not an easy or guaranteed route that I would recommend for everyone. How could I even suggest such a thing to someone who came up to me after one of my talks and said, "Listen, I'm married. I've got a family. I'm too busy making ends meet, so I can't buy a one-way ticket to India. What can I do to discover and live my passion?"

It was that question that triggered the beginning of my journey into further research to distil all the knowledge around the topic of living passionately into a practical system that helps people transform their lives. The result was several programmes around discovering and living your passion, and the most practical of them is the book you are holding in your hand.

When the voice and the vision on the inside is more profound, and more clear and loud than all opinions on the outside, you've begun to master your life.

—John Demartini

WHY Should You Even Listen to Me?
As great as this might sound, it was one thing deciding what I wanted to do and an entirely different thing making it happen!

Since my return in 2013, I invested all my time, energy, and efforts into studying and researching the topic of passion. I looked into every book that was ever written as well as every programme and training course. I learned different human behaviour sciences and gained qualifications in various coaching techniques from the world's greatest thought leaders.

By 2016, I launched Passion Sundays, the world's leading passion talk show, where I travel the world to conduct in-person interviews of 160+ leaders, authors, speakers, coaches, celebrities, Olympians, and Nobel Prize laureates to date. My aim was to dive deep into their interpretation of passion and its impact on all aspects of success in life and work.

By end of that year, I got recognised as one of the Top 100 Coaches & Leaders of the Future, by Dr Marshall Goldsmith, the world's #1 Executive Coach. Keeping in mind that over 12,000 coaches applied for the award, this means that the acceptance ratio is less than 1%. Compare that to Harvard, which admitted 938 of 6,473 applicants last year (14% of applicants). This means it was 14 Times Harder to be Shortlisted as one of the top 100 Coaches & Leaders than to be admitted into Harvard!

One of my interviews was featured on the blog of Thinker50, the world's most prestigious ranking of the top 50 management thinkers alive.

The depth of the work done on the topic led me to co-authoring a book with Brian Tracy; being named "MR PASSION" by Prof. Tony Buzan, inventor of Mind Mapping and Nobel Prize nominee; and being named "THE PASSIONPRENEUR" by *The National*.

These years of research and study enabled me to develop an unprecedentedly deep level of understanding passion and to move from just concepts and theories into integrated end-to-end processes, tools, and techniques, which you will find embedded in this book.

Throughout the years, I have delivered hundreds of passion talks to tens of thousands of people across five continents and synthesised all this knowledge into frameworks to help organisations use passion as a competitive advantage to dominate their market and also to help executives, entrepreneurs, coaches, and speakers to build their global brand so they become recognised as passionate thought leaders.

I have written this book, *Live Passionately*, for the millions out there whom I cannot reach through my talks and seminars.

I am so committed to spreading passion around the world that I have explicitly announced a BHAG—a Big, Hairy Audacious Goal—of spreading passion to 7,777,777 people.

Am I going to get to 7 million in a few years? I'm not sure how long it will take, but since I know that I have dedicated my life to this purpose, I will get there sooner or later. My philosophy is to

Live life so fully that it is a life worth dying for.

—Moustafa Hamwi

And I assure you that when you know your purpose, you will be ready to die for it because it's the only reason worth living for, and nothing else matters.

And to be clear, to #LivePassionately means taking care of all angles of life, not only work. I always have a healthy dose of adventure, nature, yoga, meditation, social work, and lots of network building on a global scale to create a Passion Tribe.

So the fundamental question I have for you is whether, or not, you want to BECOME A SUCCESSFUL PASSIONPRENEUR who is changing the world while enjoying an amazing life truly worth living.

If so, let's get you started in discovering and living your passion and living a life worth dying for!

LivePassionately

CHAPTER 2

THE GAME PLAN

Let's Get This
Party Started

Success depends upon previous preparation, and without such preparation there is sure to be failure.

—Confucius

Why Not Dive into Passion Straightaway?

Imagine you are going for a first-time trip on a rocket-ship to the moon. Would you just get on with it, or would you prefer to be well prepared?

Would you walk into an extensive workout without warming up?

You are on a journey of self-discovery, so take your time to warm up rather than just "get on with it."

In this chapter, we are going to cover a few things. First, I'm going to help you to understand the science behind the Passion Journey. Then I'm going to help you understand how to get the most out of the journey.

Then, we are going to make a celebration plan—I'm going to make some promises to you, and I would also like you to make some commitments to yourself. Then we're going to measure your current level of passion and excitement in life.

Ask Yourself a Question

What would it be like if you started living your life fully, with passion in every single area, starting today? Starting now, even if you don't know what your passion is, you're already on the journey of living a passionate life.

Let me tell you something: this journey *is* going to transform your life. I want you to go and discover your passion and then go and live a life truly worth living—one that others would give anything for!

This is something that people miss out on. We are just alive day after day; we're getting by. And this is not why we are here in this world. We were born for a reason, and once you discover that reason, you are going to be ready to die for it. Now, **that's** what I call a life worth dying for.

Now I Want You to Do Something That Might Seem Crazy...

Say "3...2...1...PASSION" out loud, from the bottom of your heart, and say it like you mean it! It may feel stupid if you're alone in a room or with a few other people. But here's the thing: if you want to succeed in life, you need to understand that the power plant does not have energy; it generates energy.

Passion and energy are going to come from you. You're going to have to generate them day in, day out, every single moment of the day.

So Is This Another "Fluffy" Passion Book?

Let's talk about the methodology and the science behind *Live Passionately*.

The first thing we work with is executive coaching. This has been built with a lot of things we learned from the man himself—the world's #1 executive coach, Dr Marshall Goldsmith. You're getting the deepest end of the most effective coaching on this planet.

We work with axiology, which is the science of human values.

We work with neurolinguistics, which is how certain words have an impact on your brain.

We work with hypnotic techniques and mindfulness and meditation techniques.

Every single element in this course has been designed with years and years of research and development behind it. So please use it to the max; juice it for all its worth!

Why Don't People Get What They Want?

Can you guess the NUMBER-ONE reason people do not get what they want? Let me tell you why. It's actually because they do **not** know what they want.

I promise you this: ***anything*** that you want in this life is yours for the taking.

However, it all starts with actually knowing what that *anything* is, exactly.

Remember walking into an ice cream shop when you were a kid and looking at all the ice cream on the shelf, thinking, "Which one do I want?" It took you *so* much time to work it out, but once you knew, you ordered with full confidence: "Give me *this* one!"

Well, here's the thing, life *is* similar.

We don't know what we want, because there are so many things out there, and we're not sure what we want. To top it all, people are always telling us what we *should* want.

However, once you gain clarity on what *you* want, it becomes easier to make it happen because clarity brings certainty. You become sure about what you want, and this certainty brings you confidence. Your confidence levels go up, and when you're confident, you take action. So guess what happens? When you take action, you become clearer on what you like and what you don't like, and you refine it, and the cycle continues.

All you've got to do is just get clear on what you want. And then you're going to get it.

This is what we're doing here in the very first few chapters of the Passion Journey. They are designed to help you gain clarity.

That being said, let me ask you a question: "Do you want success in the *mental* world or in the *real* world?" Because a lot of people think that just by visualising it and sitting and thinking about it, it's going to happen.

I'm sorry to break it to you, but that does not work. Sure, thinking is one part of it. But it's just one part. Probably the easiest part.

There are, however, **three key steps** for success in life, and these are to think, to plan, and to do. Let me repeat that: you've got to think, you've got to plan, and you've got to do. There's no getting around these three steps, my friend.

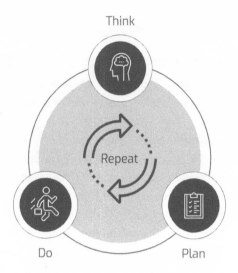

▸ To **reach goals**, make sure you do **all three**

▸ To **avoid being overwhelmed**, focus on **one at a time only**

And this is *exactly* the methodology that you will follow with the Passion Journey.

First things first. We're going to help you clarify your thinking; then we're going to help you plan, and the last thing is *you're* going to have to go and make it happen. It's a Passion Partnership!

Now I want you to know that you *are* going to get overwhelmed at times. That's perfectly normal. If you, however, want to succeed and reach your goals, you *will* have to do all three steps. Let me break this down for you and make it easier. When you feel you are getting overwhelmed, just do one thing at a time. Don't think and plan and do in one step. Do the thinking first, and then move into planning and then into doing and execution.

This Book Is Not for You

The deal-breaker here is this: this Passion Journey is NOT for you, if you are:

1. Living as a victim,
2. Not honest with yourself,
3. Close-minded, and
4. Not willing to do what it takes to put in the energy and the effort to reach your passion.

If you have checked all those as a NO, then you're all set to go!

For you to get the best and the most out of this journey, we have made this into more of a workbook, so you can do most of the exercises in it and take your notes in it too.

Before you even start on your Passion Journey, the one thing we need to do is check your mindset—that is, your levels of passion and engagement.

- Are you on top of your game? Are you passionate and fully engaged? Are you enthusiastic, energetic, and unafraid to show your level of energy?
- Or are you committed and engaged?
- Or are you just professional and doing what you have to do?
- Or are you (and this is the dangerous area) cynical?
- Or are you even hostile?

Go ahead and tick one of the boxes on the next page to know how engaged you are in transforming your life into something grander than it has always been. If you're anything less than passionate and fully engaged or committed and engaged, please stop for a moment, and ask yourself why.

Because if you are any less than passionate and fully engaged, the Passion Journey will **not** be able to help you. This is not a question of whether you should spend years trying to resolve that. You know how fast you can do it? Just close your eyes, take a deep breath, and say, "I decide to be fully present and engaged." This is as simple as it is. Just make sure you do this check.

Check Your Mindset
5 Levels of Passion and Engagement

Passionate and fully engaged

You're positive and proactive in everything you do. You feel good, and you are happy to show off your enthusiasm to the world.

Comitted and engaged

You make others feel great.

Professional

You're passively positive/politically correct

Cynical

You're bored with life, indifferent, and Superficially engage with what you are doing.

Hostile
You are proactively negative.

Now, Let's Make Your Passion Journey Fun
Why is it important to do that?

To start with, the personal development industry has suffered from becoming way too serious, and this isn't what people want or need in our stressful world.

You Learn Best When You Have Fun.

—Prof. Tony Buzan, Nobel Prize Nominee and Inventor of Mind Mapping

If you do not sprinkle some fun along the way, you're going to feel that this journey is very long and monotonous; it *will* get boring, and you *will* quit on it and want to do something more fun. So how about we make *this* the more fun thing to do?

We're all children at heart. Remember how exciting it was when you got a reward for doing something good, even if it was a little piece of chocolate or a cup of coffee? Well, when you press the reward mechanism in your brain after every step, your mind is going to collaborate with you, and this is going to help you on the Passion Journey.

Here's how we do this:

1. Give Yourself A SIMPLE REWARD AFTER FINISHING EVERY CHAPTER
Keep it simple. This could be a cup coffee, a piece of chocolate, or even something as simple as a walk. It's just about pressing the

"Well done" button in your head so you stay engaged throughout the process.

Every time I finish a module,
I will reward myself with

_____

2. Passion Celebration Sheet

This is the celebration you're going to have when you finish all the steps in this book. You are going to go out there and have fun, in whichever way you find best, because you earned it.

So, to fill the sheet, simply put a deadline for yourself to finish this book. Each chapter will take you one or two hours to go through; you could get the whole thing done in a weekend, if you like to get results fast, or a couple of months max, if you like to take things easy. It does not matter how long you take as long as you have a clear target to reach.

Put the target completion date; even better, put the time also, on the celebration sheet. Then start thinking about **where** you want to celebrate completing your Passion Journey. Just close your eyes for a moment here, and take a deep breath. Where are you when you're celebrating? Oh, it could be at home, it could be with friends, it could be in a restaurant, it could be in a club. No matter where you want it to be, just write down the place.

Then, **who** are you with? Who do you want to celebrate finding and discovering your passion with? Write down all the minor
details that come to your mind. What are you actually doing?
Close your eyes. What do you see? "Oh, I'm dancing!" Well then,
write "Dancing."

Then, **what** do you see when you're there? Look around you in
your head. You may think, "Oh my God, my whole family is celebrating. Well, I see my family celebrating with me. I hear sounds of
spoons and forks and people eating; I smell...*mmm*, warm cooked
food, and I taste...*mmm*, my favourite dish. And I feel proud and
excited that I am celebrating my passion!" Write it down, making
it as deeply detailed as you can. Conjure up the specifics, you
magician!

Then write any other descriptions that come to you. I just want the
celebration plan to be fully vivid in your head in the way that I've
just simulated with you.

Use the chart on the next page to make it vivid. Then we'll do what
it takes to make it real.

Passion
Celebration Sheet

At .... on ..../......./20.......
I am celebrating my passion.

I am at ....

With ....

Doing ....

I see ....

I hear ....

I smell ....

I taste ....

I feel ....

I ....

Now, there are four things you want to do in preparation for your Passion Celebration. Trust me, I used to organise parties for a living. So whatever I am asking you to do will ensure you have a fun journey with #LivePassionately.

So tick the boxes every time you complete one of the to-dos.

Celebration Announcement
Checklist

| Write your celebration plan | Put it on your calendar | Share it with three people close to you and ask them to hold you accountable | Share on social media that you are excited to be making a commitment to #LivePassionately |

Our Commitment

All right, I've promised you I'm going to make some commitments to you. The first, most critical commitment that I've made to myself is that in everything that I ever do in this life when I'm helping people is that I'm going to give them *immediately measurable* results.

I am adamant about the fact that it has to be immediate. Now, immediate doesn't mean in a split second. I do, however, promise for it to be faster than any other personal growth work you will ever see.

And it's measurable. So you will be able to see where you are and where you're going to be by the end of this coaching journey that we're on together. However, for us to be able to measure your success, I have to ask you a question.

What do you expect to achieve after finishing this book, after completing this journey? I want you to write down three things that you really want to achieve.

Do you want clarity? Do you want a better quality of life? Do you want to get more focused? Do you want more performance? Do you want to know what your passion is?

Please do write down the three things here.

1. ....

2. ....

3. ....

Reflect on this list for a moment. If, by the end of this journey, you do not achieve what you've written on it, please reach out to us on the Facebook group or on the support email.

I *will* do my best to help you, assuming that what you're asking for is my responsibility or within my area of expertise. Because sometimes, people expect magic to happen with the programme, but the magic has to come from *you* before it comes from me.

Having said that, I am with you *throughout* this journey.

Know Your Passion Levels

Here's one of the *most* important steps within this Passion Journey. It's what I call Passion and Motivation Clarity. Remember that discussion we had about clarity? When you're clear, you become focused, you are able to perform better, *and* your confidence goes up.

There are two questions about that that I want to ask you here.

Passion and Motivation Clarity

How clearly do you know your **passion?**

How **excited** are you about life overall?

My first question for you is: **"How clearly do you know your passion?"** On a scale from 1 to 10, 1 being, "I think I don't have a clue," and 10 being, "Oh my God, I know exactly what I'm here for, and I'm willing to die for it." I'm assuming that if it's a 10, you wouldn't be here, so you're probably in the range of anywhere from 1 to 6, 7, or even 8. We get people at a 4, but it doesn't matter where you are at. Mark where you are at today in one colour.

Now mark a target for this journey (Where do you want to be?) in a different colour. Let's say you're at a 4. Are you hoping to become a 6? Are you hoping to become an 8? Are you hoping to become a 10?

The second question is: **"How excited are you about life overall?"** Not just in relation to your passion because passion is supposed to make your life more exciting. What I want to know is how excited you are about life. Now, where are you from 1 to 10 where 1 is like, "Nah..." and 10 is like, "Yes!" Which one are you? Put a number here in one colour.

We're going to re measure those two things (clarity and excitement) by the end of this book. I can assure you something: I have never, for the past few years, since I came back from my India journey, gotten any less than a 20% increase, on average. I've had people who were at 4 and went up to 10. I've had people who were at 6 and went up to 8 and people who were 8 and went up to 10, but I rarely ever get any less than a 2-point increase. I say this with the certainty that I do not know of anything in this world that can guarantee you and offer you so much.

There *is* a catch here. The gap between where you are and where you want to be is related to how much energy, effort, dedication, and focus you—and I mean *you*—are willing to put into this programme. Of course, I am going to do my best, but it takes two to tango. You're the one who's going to do the work; I'm going to be with you.

All right? Deal?

Wheel of Life

People put too much effort into "I want to turn my passion into a business," and that's great. But guess what? In the studies that we've done so far, there are eight key areas in life that you need to balance to be living passionately, which we will tackle later on.

You may have seen lots of different versions of the Wheel of Life in other programmes. It is a very powerful tool to use to measure where you are right now and then again when you're done with the programme. Use the Wheel of Life chart below, and give yourself a score in each of those areas of life, from 1 to 10 (10 being the best).

Give yourself a score out of 10 in each of these areas

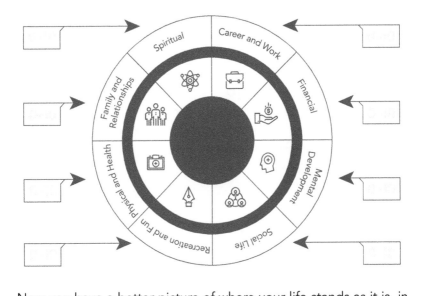

Now you have a better picture of where your life stands as it is, in totality.

Here's our second commitment to you: we're with you, step by step, until you discover and live your passion. That much I guarantee you—I'm not going to let go; I'm always going to be with you because this is a commitment and a dedication from me to you.

I have changed my life to be able to help people like you, because I never found much help when I started my journey. I will not let you come out empty-handed from this coaching programme because it's impossible to you stick your hand in a honey jar and come out empty-handed. Something is bound to stick. Sometimes, you put your hand in and take a lot out, and sometimes, you just put your hand and take whatever comes. But something will always stick.

Is that good? Deal? That's my part of it; remember, it takes two to tango.

So now to your part.

It Takes Two to Tango

Now that we've made some commitments to you, if you really want to get results, if you really want to live a passionate life, you will need to do some serious work.

So let's get started.

I want you to agree with me to **"make this self-development and not shelf-development."**

Please say it out loud, as loud as you can!

Why? Do you know those people who do a training course or a learning programme and keep piling them on one after the other but never apply them?

Guilty as charged! I did this for years and years before I learned that if I don't apply it, nothing would work. **Knowledge is power only when applied.** Thus, the five things I need you to keep in mind in every step of this programme that we're working through are:

1) Be present, and be here. That's why some of the preparation is that I ask you to turn your phone, your email, and your social media off. Because if you're not here, you're not here. You're somewhere else, and you're wasting your time, and, in that case, I urge you to just stop reading this book and doing this programme. Go do something that's more important for you. That is, *if* there is something more important than growing in your life and finding your passion.

2) Manage your energy. Everybody's got different energy levels. Nobody is better than others; you've just got to know your body type. Are you the kind of person that likes to push, push, push? Or do you like to pace yourself? I'm the kind of person that likes to sit down and do everything in one go, to just keep on going and then take a long break. Some people like to pace it and like to be slow. Just make sure your energy is always up, and if you feel the energy's not there, do whatever you have to do. Get up, walk around, shuffle things up, and manage your energy.

3) Keep moving. What do I mean by keep moving? You will be overwhelmed, you will be stressed, you might get anxious. This is not just a journey; it's an inwards journey where you're discovering yourself. That's why you're going to feel overwhelmed, and every time there's an overwhelming sensation coming your way, what I will need you to do is to take a deep breath and just keep moving on.

4) Be intuitive. What does that mean? I don't want you to sink into one of those, "Oh my god, I don't know the answer" moments and stop. You see, the pace at which I'm running this with you is important. I want you to just keep moving, which means that if you feel you're spending too much time in your head, just take a deep breath, and write the first answer that comes to mind. Here's the thing: you can change your mind later. Even if you don't like what you wrote, you can come back to it later. However, it's better to write something and change it later than to stop and try to make it perfect. Because it's never going to be perfect; all you've got to do is just keep on moving on.

5) Enjoy! Enjoy, enjoy, enjoy. Have a big smile on your face. I've put a smile for you on every single page in the top corner. This is how important it is, because I was guilty as charged of making my personal development journey so harsh and so heavy on the head that my heart was drying out. This is life; this is *your* life. Enjoy every single moment of it.

All right? Deal.

I *am* going to remind you of these things, by the way, with every module.

Your Mantra

The next thing I want you to do is to repeat this mantra...**loud**. Please. I know I'm not there to hear you, and you may well be alone. Just trust me when I ask you to repeat this loudly. Put your right hand up and say,

> I am the master of my destiny, not a victim of my history.
>
> —Moustafa Hamwi

Go on. Say it again, "I am the master of my destiny, not a victim of my history."

Then say, "**I have courage, humility, and discipline**."

This is important, and I'm going to pause through this for a moment. Think carefully. If you are living as a victim, you're never ever going to find your passion *or* be able to live a passionate life. You *have* to keep saying it to yourself. I emphasise that because, even though I've said this a thousand times, each time I say it, I *still* feel the same level of energy come up. "I am the master of my destiny!" Oh. My. God. HOW powerful is this?

What does courage mean, really? Courage doesn't mean to have courage against the world. It means having the courage to look in the mirror and face yourself, to understand where your shortcomings are, be honest about them and have the humility to say, "Please, I need help" or "I'm Moustafa, and I need help. Even with my passion, I need help."

If it wasn't for the people who helped me, I wouldn't be where I am today. If I'm going to close my mind and let my ego become too large, I'm never going to grow. Remember, teachers are always students first. I'm the biggest student in this world, and I will be till the day I die. Make sure you have the humility to ask for help. I know you have enough of it in you to have picked up this book and to want to go the course and work through it.

Discipline, discipline, discipline. If there's one area of life that people fail at, it's discipline. I'm going to explain this to you as part of the definition of passion. If you don't have the discipline to continue with this course, I bet you that you will start with the first module, *maybe* go onto the second module, and then you're never going to touch this again.

Make It Self-Development, Not Shelf-Development.

—Moustafa Hamwi

Please repeat this: "I'm the master of my destiny, not a victim of my history. I have courage, humility, and discipline."

That being said, you are responsible for the results. Not me, *you*. I *am* here doing the best I can to help you, but if you don't do the work, you are *never* ever going to get results.

Interested in Finding Your Passion?

Let me ask you another question: "Are you *interested*, or are you *committed*?" If you're interested, put your hand up and say, "I'm interested." If you are "interested," I would urge you to go to the movies and not read this book!

You know why? Because being "interested" is something that you do when you're there to just watch, observe, and say, "Maybe I like it, maybe I don't." There's nothing wrong if you started this book being just interested; that's a good start. However, you're not going to be able to climb the highest mountain in the world when you are just "interested."

You *have* to be committed. And the Everest we're about to climb is *inside* you. This is your own Everest, and *that* takes commitment. So if you said, "I'm interested," that's okay. Just put your hand up, and take a really deep breath and really be convinced that you are ready to be **committed.** You have to understand that you *cannot* be a tourist on your own Passion Journey.

The next commitment I need you to make is to say, **"I will live through to the passion that I find during this book, and I will do what it takes to make it happen."**

Please do say it loudly. I know; entertain me. Maybe I'm asking for too much at the beginning, but this is very important. I've always learned from one of my teachers and mentors that a short pencil is better than a long memory. And although we've made these commitments verbally, when you put pen to paper, things are totally different.

I ....

hereby declare that

I am a .... of my ....,
not a .... of my history.

I have ...., ...
and .... I am ....
not just interested.

I will be fully ....
I am responsible for my results, I know that I ....
What I .... in. I will .... to my
passion that I find during this programme and will
.... to make things ....

Go ahead. Sign this declaration sheet. When you do this, you will have just put pen to paper before God, the Creator of the universe; the world; and yourself.

I don't care what you believe; you *have* made a commitment, and you better live through it. Because I promise you, if you don't, you're going to feel very bad inside, and you're going to look back on your life and regret *not* following through on these things.

All right, deal!

The next thing I want you to do is just this. I know I've asked you for a lot, so take a deep breath, and do this one other critical thing. I want you to set your intentions for this programme. Because our intentions create our reality. I want you to just visualise and close your eyes. We've made all these commitments; you understand how things are set up, and the plane is about to take off. So just set the intention, and say, **"My intention is to come out of this programme truly passionate, at least 10%–20% more than when I started."**

Time to Reward Yourself, Well Done!

#Live Passionately

CHAPTER 3

THE PURSUIT OF HAPPINESS IS MAKING YOU SAD

So Let's Talk about What Passion Really Means

Happiness is not a goal. It's a by-product of a life well lived.

—Eleanor Roosevelt

New Results Require a New Mindset

All of us are pursuing the holy grail of "passion." However, I can assure you most are not even clear what passion really means. It is one of the most manipulated words in the world, yet once we clear the confusion, your motivation is going to go through the roof because you will finally get the understanding that will allow your heart and mind to become friends.

The Pursuit of Happiness Is Making You Sad

Let me ask you a question: "Do you want to be happy?"

I guess the answer is yes?

Do you want to be happy *all* the time? This is where the answer starts varying. Some people say, "Yeah"; some people say, "Not really."

If you said yes, you want to be happy all the time, I'm sorry to break it to you: you're never going to be able to be happy all the time. Why? Because life is about sometimes being happy, sometimes being okay, and sometimes being not so happy.

It would be very difficult, wouldn't it, to be happy if somebody hit my car or if I lost some money or if something went wrong with my life? It wouldn't define me in that moment, but I wouldn't actually be feeling happy.

You see, life is built on concepts. One of the popularly known, and age-old, concepts of life consists of the yin and the yang.

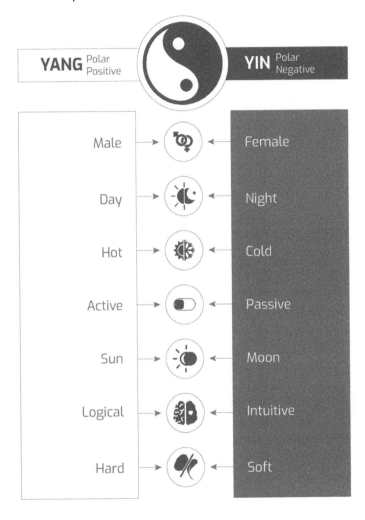

I'm sure you've seen the sign before, but do you actually know what it means?

Yin and yang are two forms of energy. They are the two polarities of life: the polar negative and the polar positive.

Yin is the softer energy; it is the intuitive female energy. It's the night, it's the cold, it's the passive, and it's the moon.

Yang is the "polar positive." It's the male, it's the day, and it's the sun. It's hot, it's active, and it's logical. Yin and yang complement each other because we human beings are not either-or.

Let me be clear why I'm calling it "the polar negative" because one time I said this in a room full of ladies, and when I said, "Negative is female," everybody went crazy on me. I said, "Hold on. It's the 'polar' negative. That doesn't mean bad or good; it's not that the positive is better than the negative." Okay, got it?

Think about a magnet. Have you ever seen a magnet with one side? Even if you break a magnet, the two halves both have positive and negative sides. In a battery as well, you've got the positive and the negative. This polarity is needed for life to move on.

Now here's an interesting thing about the pursuit of happiness. I'm telling you your pursuit of happiness is making you sad. Do you know why? If you keep trying to be happy all the time even though it's not possible, what's going to happen? You're going to naturally attract the polar opposite of happiness, which is sadness, and if you keep pursuing happiness, you're going to bring sadness into your life.

I'm not saying that you should go pursue sadness so that you can get happiness, but the one thing you've got to understand is that, in every situation in life, you have both. It's impossible to have a sun without the moon. If you've had a drink one night, you're going to have a hangover the day after. This is the nature of life. If you eat food, you're going to have to go dispose off the leftovers.

You need balance and equilibrium. And if you are pursuing happiness, it usually comes from catering to your desires.

The reality is that your desires are endless, because when you desire something, you're going to desire something else, and when you like something, you're going to want something more. This is the nature of humanity. We like more and more and more, so if the pursuit of happiness is related to desires, and desires are endless, how much wood is enough to feed the fire? It's been said that happiness is finding a scratch for every itch, and people are in eternal slavery to the monkey mind that keeps coming up with new itches that need scratching!

Did you ever think about that? We go on in our life, wanting more of everything and wanting more and more and more. This is something I suffered earlier. Before I transformed my life, I was in a business that was offering me a lot of the joys of life. Don't get me wrong; they were fun when I was doing them, but suddenly they left me more and more and yet more…empty.

What does that mean? Does that mean we should not be happy?

What Is More
Important Than
Happiness?

So What Is More Important Than Just Being Happy?

I'm not saying you shouldn't be happy. I'm just saying there's something a little bit more important than just being happy. Do you know what that is? Take a guess. I know you're going to throw out certain words. But what do you think is more important than happiness?

It's "fulfilment." Why is fulfilment more important than happiness?

Let me explain it to you linguistically, to start with. The word "fulfilment" is made up of three syllables: ful-fil-ment. Let's break it down, that's "full," "fill," "ment." Let's take off the suffix at the end—the "ment" part. That leaves us with "full" and "fill." If you invert those syllables, you get "fill" "full". So to "full" "fill" is to actually "fill" "full" that which you perceive and feel is empty inside of you.

So your fulfilment in life comes from honouring your innermost calling. When you've got a calling and you fill that calling fully, you become fulfilled. The more you fulfil your mission, the more you will feel fulfilled.

You see how this is different from happiness? The more you try to be happy, the more you feel you're empty. On the other hand, the more you try to fulfil your mission on earth, the more you will feel fulfilled. And the more fulfilled you are, the more you will fulfil of your mission. As you become more fulfilled, the world becomes better.

Isn't this amazing? I promise you, if you just get this concept deep inside your heart and mind, your life is going to change. Because, you see, all of us are walking through life wanting to feel really special.

Would you like to feel like one in a million? One in 10 million? One in 100 million? One in 200 million? How about one in 300 million? One in 500 million? You are one of 500 million other possibilities. Did you ever stop for a moment and reflect on that?

You Won Over
500 Million
Others!!!

Why did you want
to be here so badly?

#LivePassionately

One in 500 Million

There were 500 million other possibilities that could have been you. Another version of you could have come on this planet and done something totally different. But you, you, you, you, the way you are today, with everything that's going right or wrong in your life, came into this world with so much determination and so much power that you won over 500 million other possibilities.

Did you ever stop to ask yourself why? What is it that you wanted so badly that made you want to be here today?

If that is not passion, I don't know what is. And when you know what it is that you want on this planet, you come to the second-most important day of your life. Because the two most important days of your life are the day you were born and the day you find out why.

Why Should I Even Pursue Passion?

Some people ask why I need to use passion, and I hope you're not asking that question by now, but I'm going to help you clarify that.

First, **why is pursuing passion so important**?

Now, there's a possibility that you may have received this book as a gift. You might even be here because you're still interested. I want to make sure you're still committed.

When you understand why pursuing passion is so important, you're going to make more commitments towards that.

- The first reason is that **passion is energy**. Understand *that*. When you don't know your passion and pursue it, you feel a lack of energy, you feel demotivated, and you feel like you're not able to achieve your goals. When you're passionate about something, you get so much energy that people actually ask you, "Oh my God, where did you get all this energy from?"

- The second reason is that **passion brings a joyful, competitive advantage**. Let me explain to you what that means. When you are competing with somebody and both of you are doing the same business for money, time gets tough, no matter what you do. Everybody goes through tough times. The person who's in it just for the money is eventually going to get tired and try to find something else, so their performance is going to deteriorate further and further.

- But guess what? If you're just having fun and you keep playing just because you're having fun and it's your passion, I guarantee you that, over time, you *will* win. If you don't believe me, think about children. When they're playing, they just want to play more and more and more, but they don't want to do homework. So if your life becomes homework, you're going to perform less. When your life is about passion, you're going to have a lot more fun!

- The third important reason why you should pursue passion is that **passion enhances performance**. Because when you've got that much energy and you're having fun, you're going to work at it (the thing you're passionate about) better, and you're going to get better at it than anybody else. You're going to put in the hours so you're better than anybody on this planet.

- The fourth reason is that **pursuing passion increases clarity**. You remember what we said about clarity? Clarity means focus. When you're focused, you succeed better.

How many of you are struggling to stay focused on one thing? When you know what you're truly passionate about, everything starts guiding you in that direction. Think about lasers: Why is a laser so strong while light shoots off in every direction? Why is a laser so focused that it can cut diamonds? This is how much focus you're getting when you're living passionately.

- Passion also means **better decision-making**. From interviewing some of the most successful people in this world, I have found that the one thing they all have in common is that they are sharp decision-makers because they are clear. And when you're passionate, you become clear, and you make better decisions.

What Is Stopping You from Pursuing Your Passion?

Do you all agree that it is really important to live fully and with passion in every area of your life?

Because, *this* is why you're born.

Yes, we can all agree to that. The question is this: "A you actually living fully in every area of your life?"

My bet is that while most people answer yes to the first question, "We *should be* living fully and passionately," they answer no to the second question, "We *are not* living fully and passionately."

Can I ask you why? The most common answers I get are "I don't have time" or "I have children" or "I have other commitments to take care of" or "I don't know what my passion is."

Whatever your answer is, it's called an excuse.

You know why? You know why we come up with these excuses? They are a mask for fear: the fear of negative what-ifs. What if I fail? What if I don't succeed? What if they hate me? What if, what if, what if...

You *have* to wake up. You have to wake yourself up before you wake up one day and find there isn't enough time for you to do the things that you want to do in life. We don't know if we're going to be here tomorrow. What are *you* waiting for?

Most people are living their life torn between their heart and their mind, and that's **not** any way to live. Living passionately means that your heart and your mind become friends.

You see, your mind tells you about the things that you *need* to live by—that is, how to make a living. But your heart tells you about the things that are *worth dying for*. Real life is somewhere in between these two.

It's not a question of either-or; it's not a question of whether I have to slave for my entire life or let go of everything in life and just pursue what my heart is telling me.

You need to pursue what your heart tells you to get direction, but you need to use your mind in this world to be able to succeed, so please use both, and work with both.

Living Passionately
means your heart and mind become friends.

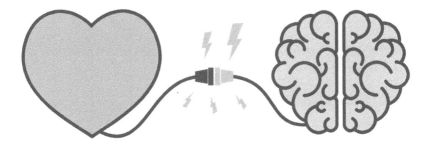

What Does Passion Really Mean?

Most people talk about passion, but not many know what it truly means!

It is one of the most abused words in the dictionary, just like the word "love." Such words touch a deeper part of us and thus require a deeper dive to understand their meaning. So as I started my research journey, I had to start with the definition of the word.

Let's start with the dictionary definition of passion: [pash-uh n], any powerful or compelling emotion or feeling.

It comes from the Latin root word "passio," which literally means "to endure" or "to suffer." Think the *Passion of the Christ*.

I guess you did not see that coming. People think passion is something that comes to you while, on the contrary, passion is that which you are willing to suffer for and endure pleasure and pain in the pursuit of, and in this way, you bring passion to life.

So we can come up with this starting-point definition of passion:

Doing what you love.

You have to be able to do what you love and/or love what you do; it's a two-way street.

I went on interviewing global thought leaders to see if this definition was solid enough to stand the test. When I interviewed Brian Tracy, one of the world's leading success experts, he said to me, "You will *never* feel passionate about something that you are not good at."

Understand that. I know you might not be good at the thing you're passionate about already, but if you're not good at it and you're working towards being good at it, your passion *is* going to increase.

But let's say you're a singer. If you keep getting on stage without any practice at all and you end up sounding like a goat, with people booing you off stage, even throwing rotten tomatoes at you, you're *not* going to stay passionate.

If you work at it and get better at it, you will stay passionate about it.

So the definition of passion evolved as I progressed with the research. It became,

Doing what you love and what you are good at.

Then, one day, I was interviewing Fons Trompenaars, the author of *Riding the Waves of Culture.* Fons is a leading author, coach, speaker, and consultant. He ranked as a Thinker50 (one of the top 50 modern-day management thinkers alive).

We were having this discussion about passion, and he said, "Be careful. The wrong kind of passion can hurt the world."

Shocked, I asked him, "The wrong kind of passion? What do you mean? There *is* no wrong kind of passion. I'm passionate, and all passion is good."

He raised an eyebrow and asked, "Really? Think about Hitler. He was doing what he loved, and he was really good at it. But it was not good for the rest of the world."

This is when it struck me that the quality of your passion comes from the quality of your purpose. One can be passionate about the wrong things as well; extreme dictators had passion, and terrorists have passion, but it's the wrong kind of passion.

If passion drives you, let reason hold the reins.

—Benjamin Franklin

So the definition of passion became,

Doing what you love and what you are good at as well as what is needed and is of service to the world.

However, when I started working for companies for a while, something was still missing. I would go to companies, I would teach all this, I would give them all this energy, and I would come back. But suddenly, the passion vanished.

I remembered something in the mantra that my mentor and coach, Dr Marshall Goldsmith, had given me. "I have courage, humility, and (the third but hardest thing out of all of them) discipline." Really, it's the discipline it takes to pursue your passion that determines if it is real passion or not. Everybody would like to do the things that they love. Everybody has certain talents that they were given; everybody wants to be of service to the world, but not everybody is consistent at it.

So to give you a practical definition of passion that we have distilled from years of helping leaders work and live passionately,

Passion is consistently doing what you love, what you are good at, and what is of value to the world.

— Moustafa Hamwi

So if it doesn't tick all these boxes, I'm sorry but it's not passion. You can call it anything else that you want, but I promise you that it's not passion.

True Meaning Of **Passion**

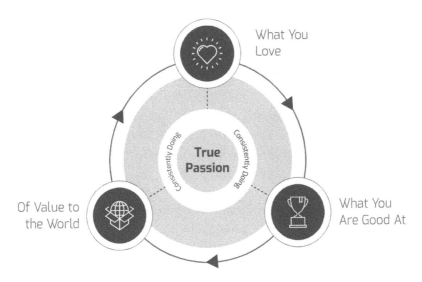

If you don't believe me, think of your schooldays.

We all had a friend who was passionate about some form of music, maybe guitar. Or it could have been a sport also. They said, "I'm passionate about music, I'm passionate about basketball." Fast forward 10–20 years, and they're not much better than when they started. So what they were saying was, "I like basketball. I like guitar. And I like to watch other people who are truly passionate about it, because I feel I'm as good as they are when I'm watching it." The reality is that only those people who are consistently working at it are truly passionate about it.

One common thing I also realised from all these interviews—160+ Passion Sundays interviews with authors, speakers, coaches, Olympians, Oscar winners, Nobel Prize winners, and other highly successful people—is that passionate people do not wait in the sidelines.

Passionate people do not wait for life to happen to them; they happen to life.

— *Moustafa Hamwi*

If you are truly passionate, you're not going to wait for passion to happen to you or to dawn on you. You're going to find it, and you're going to stay consistent; you're going to go at it, go at it, and go at it until it really comes to life.

As I said to you, passion is really not an optional thing. You were born with passion—to be passionate and to live passionately on this planet.

The best example I can give you of true passion is a tree. Why? Because a tree lives its passion and its purpose. It gives you shade; it gives you fruits; and even when it dies, the wood is of service to the world. You don't get more passionate and fulfilling than a tree.

Understand that this is the level of passion that you need. What happens when you do not do what you are meant to do in this life? If you're a fruit and you don't serve the world, either by giving the seeds or being eaten, you rot. And I'm sure none of us wants to be in this world to rot.

I know a lot of people out there are feeling like this every day. They're feeling like their life has just become monotonous, and they are now questioning the very purpose of their existence.

That's *not* the way to live. The way is to live is with full passion every single day.

Let me reveal another interesting result of my research to you. As I mentioned earlier, the word passion comes from the Latin word "passio." "Passio" means to suffer and endure. In short, that means that passion involves intense suffering, endured with self-control and tolerance. That which you are willing to endure pleasure and pain in the pursuit of is what brings you fulfilment and makes you passionate.

Passion is not just about sitting and imagining that things are going to come your way because passionate people do not wait for life to happen to them. They bring passion to life. They fulfil it no matter what comes their way.

In the pursuit of passion, there's going to be joy and pain; there's going to be happiness and sadness. But passion is not about either of them; it's about staying consistent day in, day out.

Passion Is Not Only Waving Your Hands

Do remember that very relaxed and non expressive people can be very passionate; cultural differences and styles come into play here. It's very important that you decipher what passion means to you. It's not only about waving your hands, and it's not only about experiencing emotions.

Passion comes from the heart. It's not only expressed physically; it's expressed in how you live your life.

Values and Passion

When your inner voice becomes stronger than the outer voices in the world, you become passionate because you become unstoppable. How can somebody stop you from doing what you are meant to do on this planet? You are meant to fulfil your passion.

How can anybody stop you from doing that? The only one who's stopping you is *you*. What we're going to help you do now is understand *your* values because when you understand your values, you're going to start understanding your passion.

Why?

Let me explain what the word **"value"** means. To value is to set something as a priority. When you value something, you experience that primary feeling that motivates you to do something. Values determine how people choose and determine what actions they take. Think about it. If something is high on your value system, you act with certainty. You are focused; you say things like I want, I can, I like. You are inspired from within; you are excited.

Acting from

High Value VS Low Value

✔ Certainty and quick decision	✔ Uncertainty and slow decision
✔ Focused	✔ Scattered and unfocuse
✔ I want, I can, I Like	✔ I cant, I don't, I don't like
✔ Inspired from within	✔ Motivated from within
✔ Excited	✔ Frustrated

And when something is low on your value system, you face uncertainty. You are slow in decision-making; you say things like I can't, I don't, I don't want, or I don't like. You're only motivated from without. It's not inspiration; it's external motivation. You feel frustrated.

Apply this example to food. What is a food item that you really, really like? If I come to you at any time of the day and tell you, "Let's eat this food," what's your answer going to be? "Yes, let's do it."

Now think about a food item that you really dislike. You can't even think about it. Imagine that all your friends whom you really care for and love decide to go and eat that specific food. What's your reaction going to be? You're going to be slow, thinking, "I don't really like this food, but I like my friends." There's a clash between what's high and low on your value system. You might say, "I don't want to go there, guys. Do you mind if we go somewhere else?" You feel frustrated; you have to have external motivation to do this thing with your friends. This is the simplest example I can give you that illustrates high values versus low values.

Now, understand that the hierarchy of your values determines how you perceive and act in the world. What's high on your value system will come first, and what's low is going to get pushed back. Depending on this, you're going to end up writing your destiny.

Destiny is not something that happens by itself. You are destined to fulfil your passion when you take action towards that passion based on how you value certain things in life. Does that make sense?

And when you do not fill your life with high-priority things, it will automatically get filled with low-priority things. Because if you do not know what's high on your priority system, guess what's going to happen? Naturally, you're going to turn to whatever is around you and whatever is available. That's the equivalent of junk food; I call it junk time. You're just going to spend your time doing junk tasks, and you will end up with junk time.

Do you want to know how to live a life that is full of fulfilment? Let's use this example. Let's say you have a dollar, and I want to give you euros in exchange for your dollar. Whatever the exchange rate is, I'm going to offer you three options. For every dollar, I'm going to give you half a euro, or one euro, or two euros. Which one would you like? I mean if we're smart enough, we're going to say two or more, because we want the maximum possible value for our dollar. So for each dollar, I want two or more euros.

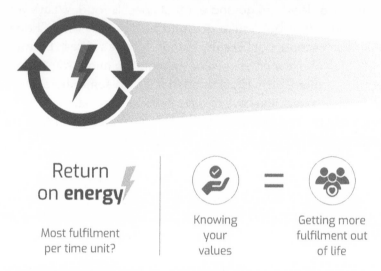

Return on **energy**		
Most fulfilment per time unit?	Knowing your values	Getting more fulfilment out of life

Now, swap every dollar for a unit of time. It could be an hour, it could be a minute, or it could be a day of your life. And swap every euro for a unit of fulfilment. Using the same analogy, how much fulfilment would you want for every single time unit you've got? How much fulfilment do you want for every day of your life?

How much fulfilment do you want? Do you want half the fulfilment, one unit of fulfilment, or two units or more?

I'm assuming the answer is going to be that you want the maximum fulfilment you can get every day of your life. That's why you're here; that's why you're even reading this book and why you're going through the course of this programme with me.

What I want you to start getting into your system is a concept: **Return on Energy**. Remember that your passion is your energy. I want you to be able to get the most fulfilment per time unit of your life. So when you know that this is high on your value system and you've got an hour to spend, spend it on what's high on your value system so that you can get more and more fulfilled.

Simply said, a more fulfilling life is about knowing your values. When you know your values, you spend your time on what you value. This is when you get more fulfilment out of life. It's that simple. Because when you know what is important, it's very easy to let go of that which is **not** important.

Makes sense?

When you know what is important, it's very easy to let go of that which isn't. Now knowing what you know, let me ask you a question: "What is more important? Time or money?" That's a tricky question because we spend and waste most of our time trying to get more money. However, understand that time is more of a diminishing resource; you're *not* going to have more time as you live. The more you live, the less time you have left.

However, there's always more and more and more money in the world because, guess what, it's just now being printed, and it's also becoming digital. Although they try to control the supply of money and make it scarce, it is *not* scarce in reality. You can wake up one day and win the lottery; you can wake up and win a million dollars. You can win a billion dollars even, but you cannot win back a minute of your life!

If you procrastinate something, can you rewind and go back and do it? No. You can wake up and get lucky with money, but you cannot get lucky with time. Please understand that time is more valuable than money. You can always get more money, but you cannot get more time.

When something becomes of high value to you, when you know that it's truly missing, not just externally but deep within, then you're experiencing that calling that I mentioned earlier. It *will* become high on your value system, and when you raise it up high, you know it's a calling. This is what a calling means; it's something that is very high on your value system. When you were the one chosen from 500 million, it was embedded in you. As it becomes your calling, it calls out to you. You become passionate about it, and when you fulfil it, you become more fulfilled.

It's that simple. If you want to raise the quality of fulfilment in your life, just trade every single time, energy, and effort unit of your life with something that truly fulfils you.

All you've got to do throughout the days of your life, moving forwards, is to keep trading in for a higher value of fulfilment!

THE SECRET TO A TRULY PASSIONATE LIFE IS TO TRADE YOUR TIME, ENERGY, AND EFFORTS FOR WHAT FULFILS YOU.

Time to Reward Yourself, Well Done!

#LivePassionately

CHAPTER 4

YOUR PASSION BLUEPRINT

Discovering Your
True Values

The two most important days in your life are the day you are born and the day you find out why.

—Mark Twain

Welcome to the second-most important day of your life.

In This Chapter

You are going to discover *your* true values and passion in a personalised manner. None of those "tick the box/multiple choice" questions for you because you are special! Every single answer will be 100% personalised for you.

Know Your Values, Find Your Passion

So for this chapter, it is very, very important that you make sure you are in your own space (your room, your office, or even a quiet corner in a park). Just make sure you take all possible measures to stay uninterrupted—*no* phone, *no* social media, *no* interaction with any other human being for just about an hour, because this chapter requires you to answer questions continuously and in an intuitive manner. So do what it takes to stay uninterrupted.

Being intuitive will be key to the success of your work in what follows. I'm going to run you through a series of introspective questions to help you gain clarity on what is valuable for you in your life.

Over the next few pages, you will see a table that has three columns and multiple line items. These are for you to jot down your answers.

For each of the questions asked, put down a total of three answers. What is important is that you answer as quickly and intuitively as you can.

Nobody is going to see these answers but you. These answers are related to you and you alone. So answer as honestly as you can.

The process works like this: you read the question, take a deep breath, and intuitively write the first three answers that come to mind.

If I ask you, "What is your favourite colour," and the first answer that comes into your mind is "apple," what answer should you write?

No, you don't write red, you don't write green. You write "apple."

Why? Because "apple" is the intuitive answer; green or red are the analytical answers. Apples come in a variety of different colours that you might not even know of. However, your analytical mind is going to interfere in the process, telling you what the mind thinks an apple "should be."

Remember, this is the kind of thinking that drove you away from your true passion in the first place.

This process is designed in a certain way to tackle your subconscious mind, and, sometimes, that *will* trigger what might seem like an illogical answer when you look at it in isolation. Just trust the process while answering. At the end of this chapter, we're going to analyse these answers to make sense of them.

To get the most intuitive answers, your mind needs to be in an "alpha" wave, which is a relaxed, reflective state: the state of being present in the "here and now." On the other hand, being in the "beta" wave is being in a highly alert and intellectual state that is ruled by what society has told you about who you can and cannot be.

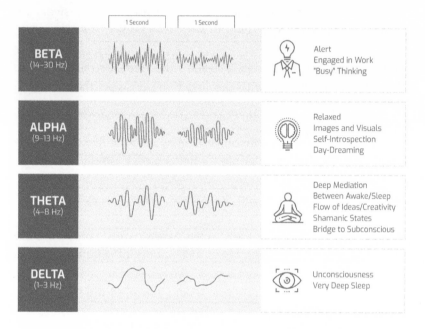

The simplest way to get into the "alpha" state is to just start with a deep breath and then write the first three answers that come to mind for each question.

If you've got one answer that is predominant—that is, the "it" answer—then repeat it in all three boxes. Otherwise, just write what comes to mind (it's more important that you move forwards with the exercise rather than getting stuck on producing three answers).

Try not to take too much time in answering because, if you do that, the answers will come from your mind, while we want the answers to come from your heart!

Let's Get Some Answers

All right, are you ready?

1. **What kind of books and magazines do you like to read or browse through?**

   ....
   ....
   ....
   ....
   ....
   ....
   ....

2. **What do you like to search the internet for?**

   ....
   ....
   ....
   ....
   ....
   ....
   ....

3. **What do you like learning about?**

   What are the things that you actually, willingly love to learn?
   These are not the things you were forced to learn at school or
   university.

   ....
   ....
   ....
   ....
   ....
   ....
   ....

4. If you were going to only watch TV for the rest of your life, what kind of content would you consume?

You can answer in terms of existing channels or something created especially for you.

....
....
....
....
....
....

5. What do you do to make your personal space unique to you?

A personal space can be your workstation, desktop, cubicle, computer desktop, living room, bedroom, and so on.

What do you put up in your personal space? Words, symbols, pictures? If they're pictures, then what do they depict?

....
....
....
....
....
....

6. Where are you most organised?

Even if you are a messy person, you are going to have a place or an area of life where you are a bit more organised.

....
....
....
....
....
....

7. What talents have you got?
These are the God-given things that you are naturally good at.

....
....
....
....
....
....
....

8. What are your "passions," as per the common understanding? What are the things that you really love doing?

....
....
....
....
....
....
....

9. What is easy for you that seems difficult for others?
Think of something that comes naturally to you whereas others go, "Oh my God, how did you do that?"

....
....
....
....
....
....
....

 Now is a good time to take a deep breath in...and out...so you can relax your mind into an "alpha" state.

10. How do you *like* to spend your time?
This is about life, in general, but if your answer is "Work," then what do you actually do at work. Do you analyse numbers? Do you write reports? Do you come up with ideas?

....
....
....
....
....
....
....

11. What activities make you lose track of time?

....
....
....
....
....
....
....

12. How do you use your energy?
When you are feeling energised, what do you do with that energy?

....
....
....
....
....
....
....
....

13. What energises you more at the end than at the beginning?
What activities make you feel more energised by the *end* rather than when you started?

....
....
....
....
....
....

14. Apart from your basic bills, what do you spend your money on?
Whenever you have spare cash—and don't tell me you don't have spare cash, *even* if it's only a dollar—how do you spend that money?

....
....
....
....
....
....

15. What are the top three things on your mind at any given point of time?
What keeps popping up in your head regularly? What are the thoughts that occupy your mental space?

....
....
....
....
....
....

16. What do you envision the most?

This question is about the visuals that come regularly into your mind. What are the things you daydream about the most and create the most mental pictures about?

....
....
....
....
....
....
....
....

17. When and where do you get your best ideas?

This is unique to each person, so give a no-holds-barred response. It could be the shower, it could be while working, and so on.

....
....
....
....
....
....
....
....

18. What do you talk to yourself about the most?

That's the internal conversation going on inside your head.

....
....
....
....
....
....
....

19. What do you talk to people about the most?
This is about external dialogue. If it was up to you, what conversation would you end up having with people?

....
....
....
....
....
....

20. Which topic gets you most animated while talking about it?
Even if you're an introvert and your body language is not that expressive, you *will* find yourself getting more animated when you're speaking about certain topics. It might be as simple as moving your hands one inch away from your body or having a small smile on your face.

....
....
....
....
....
....

21. During what activities or topics do you get excited about tiny little details?
If you love a Ferrari, that does not make you a car fanatic. If you can tell whether the screw that's on the wheel of the Ferrari belongs to it, *that* would be you being a car fanatic.

....
....
....
....
....
....

Now is a good time to take a deep breath in...and out...so you can relax your mind into an "alpha" state.

22. Which areas of work and/or life do you over deliver in?

What is so important to you that if someone asked you to do it, you would go above and beyond what is expected?

....
....
....
....
....
....

23. What do you set goals towards the most?

Are you thinking that you're not a goal-setting type of person? We are looking for things about which you express wanting regularly, with words like, "I want to..."

....
....
....
....
....
....

24. In which areas of life are you the most reliable?

These are the areas in which somebody can depend on you 110% and know that you are going to get things done.

....
....
....
....
....
....

25. What triggers your *positive envy* regularly?

I'm talking about the good kind of envy that makes you want to *work hard* to get that thing. I don't mean the kind of envy or jealousy where you hate somebody and wish them ill. Hopefully, you never do that!

....
....
....
....
....
....

26. What gives you chills regularly when you talk about it, think about it, experience it, or see it?

I'm looking for a physical reaction or a sensation you experience when exposed to a topic or situation.

....
....
....
....
....
....

27. What inspires you the most?

This could be something in life, in general, or at work, but it should be something that truly, always, never fails to inspire you.

....
....
....
....
....
....

28. What are your top three wishes?

You just found what looks like a magic lamp. The genie has appeared and offered you three wishes. What would you wish for?

....
....
....
....
....
....
....
....

Now on to my favourite question...

29. The billion-dollar question: If you had a cheque in your name for one billion dollars, what would you do for a living?

Use the cheque on the opposite page to help you with the process. Just fill in the cheque; then take a deep breath, and write the first three answers that come to your mind.

....
....
....
....
....
....
....
....

Now is a good time to take a deep breath in...and out...so you can relax your mind into an "alpha" state.

Passion Bank

Date: _____

Pay to the order of _____

$ | 1,000,000,000 |

_____ DOLLARS

Amount _____

Signature _____

⑆0 1 2⑆ ⑈34567⑈890⑆: 1234⑈567⑈

30. What would you do if you were *guaranteed* success?
Think about something that is related to a talent or a skill set, NOT something related to money or material achievements

....
....
....
....
....
....
....
....
....
....
....
....
....

31. If you could write a book that would be a guaranteed bestseller, what would it be about?
NOTE: This can be one answer that you repeat three times.

....
....
....
....
....
....
....
....
....
....
....
....
....

32. What would you do for a living if you had to work for NO money?

Imagine this. You're in a utopian community based on barter. The value of a shoemaker's service is equal to the value of a doctor's service. Everybody's needs are taken care of in this community. What would you do for a living in a community where you *cannot* make or accumulate money?

NOTE: This can be one answer that you repeat three times.

....
....
....
....
....
....
....
....
....
....
....

33. What do you want to be remembered for after you die?

What legacy do you want to leave behind?

....
....
....
....
....
....
....
....
....
....

34. If today was last day of your life, what would you regret NOT doing?

Time is a healer. Your regret for the mistakes you have made will be resolved over time. But you cannot rewind time to go back and do the things that you have not done.

....
....
....
....
....
....
....

35. What always puts a big smile on your face?

What are the things that are guaranteed to always put a smile on your face?

....
....
....
....
....
....
....

36. What are the three happiest moments in your life?

When did these occur? What were you doing at the time?

....
....
....
....
....
....
....

37. What was your childhood uniqueness?
What talents, what habits, or what words that you spoke were
you known for?

....
....
....
....
....
....

**38. When you were a little child, what did you say you wanted
to be when you grew up?**
If you can't remember, don't worry. It's not a big deal. Most people
don't. If you do, but it does not make sense, write it down anyway.

....
....
....
....
....
....

**39. What have you been working hard on developing most of
your life, even if you haven't succeeded yet?**
We are *not* looking for an area where you have already become
good. We are looking for areas where you are not that strong
but are determined to become so, no matter how many years
it will take you. These are the areas you keep coming back to.

....
....
....
....
....
....

40. What are the things about the world you would change if you had the resources?

What is it that you *really* hate about the world around you and would change, if you had the necessary resources? This has to be something very personal to you, something that you believe in deeply yourself. Remember, no cause is better or worse or more important or less important than others. So it must be something that means a lot to *you*, something that you want to fix.

NOTE: *This can be one answer that you repeat three times.*

....

....

....

....

....

....

WELL DONE! We just completed a 3-D holographic image of what you value in life and your true passions.

We have tackled questions that relate to:

- your heart and your mind;
- your past, present, and future;
- your aspirations and reality; and
- your left brain and right brain.

It's a very powerful way of digging deep and going around and through many dimensions to understand the true passions that are embedded deep in your subconscious mind.

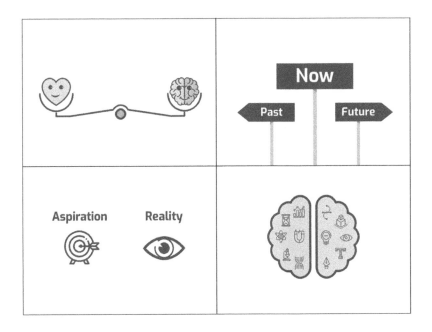

Organising Your Answers—*Word Count*

In this step, we are just going to do a simple word-counting exercise.

1. Quickly scan through the answer sheets. Do you see any trend in these answers, any words that jump at you?
2. Using the Word Count Sheet, put the words that are most repeated with the count next to them. (Make sure you tick off the words in the answer sheet as you count them, so that you do not get confused.)
3. While you count the answers, don't merge them. For example, if you have "food" and "cooking," count "food" separately from "cooking."

Word Count Sheet

NOTE: The aim is to count the majority of the keywords; do not stress about counting every single word in the answer sheet. This step should take you no longer than five minutes.

Word	Count	Word	Count	Word	Count

Grouping Your Answers: Mind Mapping

Mind mapping is a system invented by my friend and mentor, Prof. Tony Buzan. He says that our minds work in an *expansive* manner rather than in a *linear* manner. This theory even matches the way the neurons of the brain look.

In this technique, you look at a central idea that branches out into more ideas and that further branch out into more relevant ideas. It's *that* simple.

So, to do the process using the Mind Mapping sheet:

1. Take the highest-counted word from the Word Count Sheet, the thing most valuable to you, and put it in the centre.
2. Then take the set of words that have counted a little bit less, and place them on the four boxes branching out from the centre.
3. Then put words that relate to each of these words on further peripherals.

My Highest Values Are

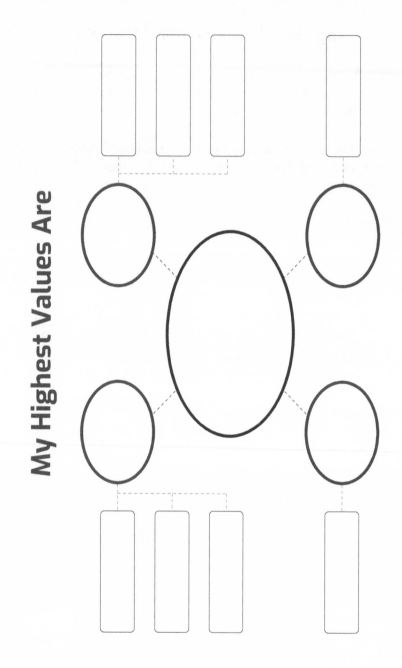

Example:

Word Count: Food, 10; cooking, 5; tomato, 2; potato, 1. Mind
Map will be

- Food
  - Cooking
    - Tomato
    - Potato
  - People

My Highest Values Are
Example

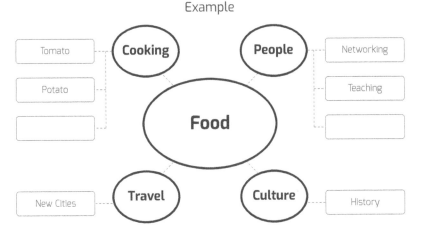

With this process, you should have your first comprehensive picture of your real value system—what you're truly passionate about
in this life!

Remember the equation we tackled in earlier chapters to give you
the most fulfilment in life? It was about exchanging every unit of
time for the maximum number of units of fulfilment. To achieve
that, starting today, every decision you make, has to be based on
two criteria:

If the answer is NO to both the above questions, then simply do NOT do it. Because it will be a total waste of your time and energy. Only when the answer is YES to both questions will you live the highest quality life you can ever live.

From today onwards,
every decision should be based on two criteria

Does it
**align with
my values?**

Does it
**move me closer
to my vision?**

Time to Reward Yourself, Well Done!

LivePassionately

CHAPTER 5

GETTING
CRYSTAL
CLEAR

Vague Passion

= Vague Results

Clarity breeds mastery.

—Robin Sharma

Getting Crystal Clear

Knowing the big picture of your passion is one thing. Making sense of it is a completely different thing.

If you found out in the previous step that you love cars, this chapter will help you understand if you want to drive cars, sell cars, do car paint jobs, sell spare parts, be a mechanic, and so on.

This chapter alone, when done with great focus and intent, will give you absolute clarity on what you want in life and will 10x your decision-making ability and the speed with which you achieve your dreams.

Investing Time

Let me ask you a question: "Do you love life?"

If you love life, do not waste time. Because time is what life is made up of.

—Bruce Lee

When you waste your time, you are wasting your life. So let's start some strategic planning for your future.

Research tells us that people increasingly *overestimate* what they can do in a year but *underestimate* what they can do in three to five years. So considering the next three to five years will give you a long enough runway to change things in your life.

Fast forward three to five years from now. Let's just assume you have 100 time points at your disposal. This could mean 100 minutes, 100 days, or 100 hours; whatever it is, it's 100% of your time.

Remember that Mind Map that we created? Please refer to that and choose how you would like to reprioritise things. How would you distribute your time to each of the nodes/peripherals? Which of the peripherals would you give most time to, which is the next most important, and so on? If you feel the need to give more or less time to any of the things on the Mind Map, or maybe even group some of them into a single activity, please do so.

Use the worksheet below to distribute these 100 points.

I will distribute
100 time points
over my passions as follows

.... time points on ....

.... time points on ....

.... time points on ....

.... time points on ....

.... time points on ....

How you distribute your time is entirely up to you; there's no right way or wrong way. Put your values on the right side and put the time points on the left side. Just ensure that the total of your time points adds up to 100.

Meaning of Work

Most people do not even understand where work fits in the whole picture of their life. Most people feel that they *have* to work to meet the responsibilities that have either been thrust on them or that they are expected to fulfil.

Let's be clear: you may be stuck in a job you don't like, but in an ideal world, what would work be for you? Would it be:

- A MISSION AND A CALLING?
  - Typically, this is something at the level of humanitarian aid and can even go so far as to be *something you are willing to die for* like solders fighting wars to protect their countries.
- FUN?
  - Having fun while you work is a priority. If you're not having it, then you would rather not work. This typically applies to the hospitality industry.
- PURELY A JOB?
  - Typically, this is for someone who feels work is a means to an end. This would be something that you would do just to make a living and take care of your family.

You can also have the "in-between," like a "joyful job" or a "joyful mission."

Let me be clear. There is no right or wrong in this, and nobody is better than anyone else. Somebody who defines work as a "mission" is not better than somebody who looks at work as purely a job. This is just the way your internal operating system works when you look at "work." Ask yourself this question, and tick the box in the worksheet on page 96.

It's important that you answer this with a lot of honesty. If you're not honest, you're only fooling yourself, and then you're going to design your life in a way that will leave you neither fulfilled nor empowered—the wrong way.

I Feel Fulfilled

Continue this sentence: "I feel the most fulfilled when I am…" Here are three possible options:

- The ENTREPRENEUR dealing with ambiguity
- The MANAGER responsible for systems and other people in an operational and functional ladder
- The TALENT—that is, the person who likes to use their own talent to do work with their own hands and get things done

To clarify this a little bit for you, none of these is better than the other. So do not be fooled by the word "talented." Do not be fooled by statements such as "This is a more talented person, and other two are not."

In the example of a restaurant,

- the talent is the chef,
- the manager is the person who manages the running of the restaurant on a day-to-day basis,
- the entrepreneur is usually the owner of the restaurant, whom *you* barely ever see, but who is trying to make ends meet in various ways without you even knowing about it.

Ask yourself, "Where am I the most fulfilled?" This doesn't mean you can't do all three; it just means that one of them is usually your biggest driver. Your response can be a mix of two, but please don't tick all three boxes in the worksheet on page 96.

Money, Power, and Fame

What is your answer to the question: "What is my game: Money? Power? Or fame?"

This does not mean you cannot have all three. And it definitely does not mean you cannot play in all three.

However, we are mostly designed to excel in our primary mode of operation. Think about a race car and a high performance 4x4. Neither is better than the other; the 4x4 will operate best in off-road conditions, and the race car will operate best on the track.

To help clarify more, here are some examples:

Warren Buffet. What do you think is his game? Is it money, power, or fame?

Well, you know what? It's money, although he is famous (for being rich) and has made a great impact on the world (power) by donating to charity rather than being part of the United Nations.

Here are some examples of people who are more about power (impactful people fit into this category): Mother Teresa, Nelson Mandela, Gandhi, the Secretary General of the United Nations, Steve Jobs, and Bill Gates. Again, none of them are "better" or "worse" than the others. This is not what we are discussing.

For these people, their game of making an impact and getting results is a game of *power*—the power of persuasion, authority, or creativity—not a game of money.

And the third kind of game is that charming old lady, Fame. Think about singers, actors, speakers, artistes, and media personalities. They're obviously into fame. They still make an impact and gather riches through their fame.

NOTE: I'm just using certain examples for the purpose of clarity. I'm not here to discuss your opinion or share mine about the people I mentioned or how good or bad they are.

You may rank these three games in a certain order, if you prefer not to choose a top one. If you do, the first one will be where you feel you are strongest.

In case you are still confused, don't worry. I'm going to help you figure out which one is yours. Simply start by eliminating which one is NOT. You'll then be left with two. Usually the confusing two are money and power.

Here's the question to give the answer to, if you get stuck for your number-one choice: "You have an opportunity to choose between a cheque for a million dollars and to be appointed president of a country; which one do you prefer?"

If you chose the cheque, then you know you're a money person, and if you chose the position, then you know you're a power person.

These three questions alone are immensely powerful in giving you clarity about yourself and how you view life:

- What does work mean to you?
- When are you most fulfilled?
- What is your game?

My Primary
Operating Model

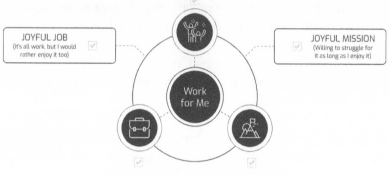

JOY
(All about the fun)

JOYFUL JOB
(It's all work, but I would
rather enjoy it too)

JOYFUL MISSION
(Willing to struggle for
it as long as I enjoy it)

Work
for Me

PURELY A JOB
(It's about the money)

CALLING AND MISSION
(Willing to die for it)

I am **most fulfilled** when I am using my gift as

The Talent

The Manager/
Team leader

The Entrepreneur/
Intrapreneur

MY GAME

MONEY

POWER

FAME

How to Get to Passionate Work

Here is where I'd like to remind you of our definition of passion: "Passion is consistently doing what you love, what you are good at, and what is of value to the world."

That being said, if you would like to turn your passion into your work, first we have to figure out three things:

- what you love,
- what you are good at, and
- what is of value to others and has a market.

What you *love* are things that make your heart pump. They get you moving, and you experience special feelings when you want to do them and when you look at them. These are the things we figured out through the 40 questions.

Now, it's time to think about which of them you are good at *and* whether that has a market—that is, a value for someone else. Once you find the intersection between all three, that is when you have found your **sweet spot.**

Look at the "The Sweet Spot Chart" below, and start thinking about your values and passions and how you want to distribute them over the three circles.

The Sweet Spot

The aim is to find the intersection between these three circles; only *that* can be passionate work. For anything that lies in the other two circles, you're going to have to invest time into moving it into the centre.

Let's say there's something that you love and you're good at, but it does not seem to have a market (this is called a **hobby**). You will need to do more market research on how you can bring it to the market, how to find the clients who are interested in it, or how to package it differently so you can sell it.

Let's say there's something that you love, and it has a market, but it's not something you're good at (this is called a **dream**). Guess what you're going to have to do. You're going to put in the hours to learn it and practice it till you get really good at it.

Let's say you're doing something that you're good at, and it has a market (this is called a **job**), but you don't love it. Then you have one of two options. Either look for something else that makes you tick or love what you are good at. It's simply about understanding that this talent was given to you for a reason!

Make Your Passion a Hobby First

So when you look at this whole picture, you're going to understand that success has a much bigger meaning. In that context, I would like you to do one thing. I want you to *start by making your passion into a hobby*. Do not rush into making it into a business. I wish somebody had told me that before I started my journey. Because once I discovered what my passion was, I was so excited about turning it into a business that I ran into roadblocks quickly, and then, I learnt the hard way. Here are a few advantages of starting with passion as a hobby *before* you turn it into a business.

- **You Learn Better**
  You learn better when you have fun. Prof. Buzan, inventor of Mind Mapping, taught me this. He actually explained the science behind it to me. We don't have time for this now, but I promise you that you will learn better when you're having fun.
- **You Experience Joy**
  You will enjoy it more when you're not under pressure to perform. Because when you take your passion from a hobby space into a professional space, you will be competing with professionals—people who have put in the

hours. You will be tempted to compare yourself to them, and there's nothing else that sucks the joy out of anything more than comparison.

It's like when you first walk into the gym and begin working out, you see a lot of people pumping iron, and you start comparing yourself to them. Guess what's going to happen? It's going to make you try to keep up with them, and you're going to lose the joy and the fun factor, or you *will* hurt yourself. (Guilty as charged; I did it too!)

- **Breathing Space**
  You have more room to explore through trial and error, because when you are pursuing your passion as a hobby first, and you make a mistake, well really, who cares?

  But if it's a profession, you *cannot* afford mistakes, because people are judging and evaluating you on it. You might be paid for it, so there's no room for trial and error. And I can't tell you honestly enough that I wish *I* knew all these things before I started.

I urge you to remember all these things before you move forwards by taking your passion and making it into a business. So start with your passion as a hobby.

How Can I Make My Passion My Profession?

I'm sure most of you would like to turn your passion into a profession. I'm going to give you the roadmap to do that. Check this out:

- When you work consistently at something, you GET GOOD AT IT.
- When you get good at it, you become a master, an expert, a PROFESSIONAL at it.
- And when you become professional at it, you can turn it into a PROFESSION.

Profession Mastery

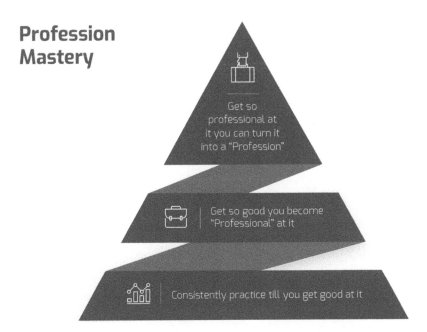

Get so professional at it you can turn it into a "Profession"

Get so good you become "Professional" at it

Consistently practice till you get good at it

This is the missing link. People try to jump from "I love it" into "I want to make it into my business" without going through the whole process. This *hardly* ever works. Never forget—you have to walk before you run, and you have to run before you fly!

Passion Mastery

So, to be able to figure that area where you can be a professional, let's look at these three circles in the Passion Mastery chart. Passion

Passion Mastery

This is what I call Passion Mastery. You've got to look at three things to be a master in any area in life.

- **Talent**: This is usually God given and comes to you easily and naturally, like if you're just born with a good voice or an athletic body. This could also include things that got developed at a young age.
- **Skills**: These are a specific set of steps that you have to take to achieve a certain result. These are acquired, not God given. You have to normally work for acquiring and honing these.
- **Knowledge**: This is the general body of understanding, information, and research around a certain topic. It is the general context of what you would like to master.

Mastery can only come from having *all three*, so you want to look for the intersection.

If you've got only one of them, then you're never going to become a master at your passion, even if that is a God-given talent. A lot of people depend on the fact that they're talented but never invest enough time to gain the skill set to become better at it or the total general understanding of it so they can develop a sense for it.

So if you've got only one of the three and are not willing to invest time, energy, and effort to develop the other two, then my advice would be not to waste your time on this. Look for something else.

You may still choose to go ahead and list down something where you only have one of these. If you are feeling rather talented and want to ignore this advice, then go ahead. I do want to point out, though, that I have seen hundreds of people waste their lives thinking they will be the lucky one who beats the system because their ego is telling them they are better than everyone else. Unfortunately, let me tell you that I've seen them become the rabbit that loses to the turtle, from our childhood stories.

If you've got two—either talent with skill or talent with knowledge—you are above average for sure. However, you're not a master yet.

You're only a master when you invest enough time to have all three circles.

By looking at everything you've found out so far, ask yourself the below questions about the intersection point between the three circles (what you love, what you are good at, and what has a market).

Number One: *Am I talented in it?* Do I at least have a glimpse of talent in that area, that I can work at to nourish and grow?

Number Two: *Do I have the skill set for it?* Am I at least investing enough time to gain the skill set, if I don't have it yet?

Number Three: *Do I have the knowledge* of that whole industry, what that industry means, what its challenges are, and how that whole industry operates? This is called context.

Success, To Me, Means...

From years of working with people on living a passionate life, I have come to realise that most of us overshoot with our passion and focus too much on turning passion into our full-time work. Aside from the previous questions about "What does work mean to you?" I *must* remind you, yet again, that *LIFE IS NOT JUST ABOUT WORK.*

Remember the Wheel of Life exercise that you did earlier, in which you gave yourself a score out of 10 in various areas of your life? What's more important is that you go and define success in each of those areas.

Take time and think about what your definition of success in each of those areas is.

- What does SPIRITUAL success mean to you?
....
....
....

- What does CAREER success mean to you?
  Does it mean being a CEO and being successful in leading bigger organisations? Do you want to be an entrepreneur?

Do you want to do your own thing outside the business arena, like being an artiste?

....

....

....

- What does FINANCIAL success mean to you?
  Does it mean having a million dollars? A billion dollars? Or does it just mean having enough money to enjoy a simple life?

....

....

....

- What does MENTAL success mean to you?
  This is a highly neglected area that people don't think about enough. Your mind is going to help you succeed and grow in life, and if you don't sharpen *that* sword, you're not going to be able to use it and fight throughout your life.

....

....

....

What does SOCIAL success mean to you?
Does it mean being well connected? Does it mean having a close group of friends that loves you?

....

....

....

- What does the definition of success in the area of RECREATION and FUN look like?

....
....
....

- What does PHYSICAL and HEALTH success mean to you? This body of yours is the vehicle that's going to carry you through life. If you don't take care of it and you neglect it in the pursuit of money, the net result will be only loss and failure. What's your definition of fit and healthy?

....
....
....

- What does success mean to you in the area of FAMILY relationships?
  How important is family time, and how do you define success in this area? Are you willing to sacrifice relationships with family and loved ones in exchange for success in other areas? A lot of people are!

....
....
....

Must Haves

Distribute the passions that were on the sheet we found so far and anything else you'd like to add into three categories.

- Things that I surely want a lot of.
- Things that I want a bit of.
- Things that I would like to maybe have one day.

It could be that you are looking for a lot of nature and a lot of adventure. Then make it clear that this is high priority. (Remember our discussion about priorities?) For example, I love personal growth, and I love growing my mind, so for me these things fall under "surely want a lot of."

Then the next thing on the list is things you want a bit of. So let's say you like personal development and growth, but you don't want to turn it into a business. You list that down here. Perhaps personal growth and development could be here for you!

WANT LIST

SURE WANT A LOT	WANT A BIT	MAYBE/ONE DAY

Then the "one-day/maybe" list could include writing a book. For me, writing a book ranks high on my priority list. Other people may think, "Perhaps some day, when I've fulfilled all my responsibilities, it could be something I do."

It's important that you get into different shades of passions. Remember this is not a black-or-white discussion.

No-Nos

Equally important is the no-no list. A no-no list is a list of things you surely do not want in your life.

As important as knowing what you want is knowing your boundaries—that is, what you don't want. If you don't know this, you're going to get pulled in many directions.

So what are the things that you're not willing to do?

The obvious things are ones that are not legal and ones that are not ethical. Let's say you want to make a lot of money but you don't want to make a lot of money trading arms. That might be a legal business if you're selling the arms from an official manufacturer to the military, but in your value system, that might not be what you want to do. So you're going to write that on your no-no list; this will help you to make decisions faster, especially if you are forced into certain situations that offer you opportunities that look a bit confusing.

No-No List

Things I am not willing to do/I do not want in my life for sure

- -

- -

- -

- -

- -

- -

Quality Questions

I'd like to share something I've learned from working very closely with Dr John Demartini of *The Secret*. It is that to get a good answer you have to ask a good question! It's that simple.

Life is like an open-book exam; the answers are all there. If you're not fulfilled with the quality of your life, guess what? This means you are not asking yourself the right-quality questions.

If you look back at it, all I've done with you in the past chapters is ask you a series of well-designed questions.

It took us a lot of time to design the questions, but we know those questions were triggering the right answers, and you've seen the results.

To increase the quality of your life, I'm going to give you a set of predesigned questions to help you come up with a question that you should ask yourself daily.

- How can I make my passion into more than a hobby so I can enjoy my life more?
- What do I need to study/research to get closer to my passion?
- How can I get paid to do what I love?
- How can I find a career in this field or close to it as a start?
- How can I create a business around it?
- How can I ....?

You get the gist. I'm sure you can design your own question now!

Remember, you need to design a question that you're going to ask daily. You're going to have to keep nagging yourself with this question every single day to be able to get the right answers.

Time to Reward Yourself, Well Done!

#LivePassionately

CHAPTER 6

THE
PASSIONATE
LIFE DESIGN

Life is not about discovering yourself. Life is about creating yourself.

—George Bernard Shaw

Your Dream Life, For Real

In this chapter, I'm going to help you understand the keys to designing a passionate lifestyle. Then you will draft your **Passion Statement,** which will become the North Star for your passionate life, moving forwards. And last, we're going to help you design your ideal day and your ideal weekend.

Stop Searching, and Start Living

Up until the last chapter, we were in "discover" mode. Beyond this point, there will be no more discovery work, because you will be in the "living" mode. This is where all new discoveries happen while you continue to grow. Otherwise, if you keep searching, you will be stuck in the mind game of always looking for something!

The best way I can explain it is this: in the first few modules, we dug out a raw diamond—the one that you got from the Passion Discovery chapter. This is a raw diamond in the circle. It's raw, but it's still a diamond. In the Passion Clarity chapter, we took that diamond, and we cut it, so it started looking a bit better, and you understood a little bit more about your passions.

In this chapter, which is the Passionate Life Design chapters, we're going to take this diamond and decide how it fits into a piece of jewellery. For example, we might share the exact same passions of nature, personal growth, and adventure. However, the way I

THE PASSIONATE LIFE DESIGN

design them into my life will look totally different than the way you would do it.

This is what this module is going to do for you—help you design how to fit your values and passions into your life.

Keys to a Passionate Life Design

There are certain key elements for lifestyle design. These are:

1. **Being True to Your Values**
   This includes being true to and living your values. Arrange your life in a way that allows you to focus on what is truly important to *you* so you can say "no" to what is not.

2. **Simplifying and Creating Space**
   If you want to get everything you want in life, you have to simplify your life. You CANNOT get **everything** in life, but you CAN get **what you want** in life. EVERYTHING is a lot and, in any case, most of it consists of things that you probably do not care about. So why clutter your life!

   This will also give you freedom and room to grow, so you can build your life around your passions. De-clutter your life in the areas mentioned in the Wheel of Life.

3. **Developing Positive Habits**
   This includes continually improving yourself, working towards personal mastery, and awakening to your potential.

The simplest way I can phrase this is: create a lean and fat-free life.

Your Passion Statement

Many years ago, when I started on my own journey of passion discovery, I discovered that my top values were personal development, health and wellness, adventure travel, and nature. Those were my top four values, two of which you can see inter-relating with each other.

What I did next, after finding my top four values, was to go on and write down my Passion Statement. (At that time, it did not have a name. It was just a statement of what I wanted in life once I had clarity on what was important to me.)

You can see an image of the actual document with my less-than-impressive handwriting.

I wrote this around late 2011. By then, my home country, Syria, had erupted in civil war. I was on crutches because of a lower back injury that made it impossible for me to move without aid and painkillers for a few months. (This was one of the very few times, post 2008, that I took any medicines). My career was not looking any brighter than the rest of my life.

It was almost impossible for me to imagine anything inspiring in my life. And yet, I wrote it with shaky handwriting and tears in my eyes—tears of fear and desperation. I am sharing this because I want you to remember that, no matter what the circumstances, if you set your sights on something and write it down, there's nothing that can stop you from achieving it.

So this was written in 2011. I want you to notice some keywords there.

- A life that is full of experiences
- in a way that inspires others and
- helps them to truly be who they want to be.

Fast forward three and a half to four years—April 2015 to be exact, when I delivered a talk at a school in Jordan. Interestingly, it was for teachers, not students. I was **so** worried about speaking to teachers about passion; after all, they are already serving their mission in the world! Somehow, I managed to finish that event. Imagine my absolute surprise when, after the event, the principal of the school sent a thank-you letter to the training company who had booked me!

When I got that letter, I kept reading it over and over again and saying, "No, no, no, it cannot be. Maybe I'm imagining it; it's not true."

The terminology in the thank-you letter sounded very familiar, as though I had read it before. The chatter in my mind did not stop until I dug out an old piece of paper that had my original Passion Statement from 2011, and I put both documents next to each other.

I want you to carefully read the scan of that letter, and observe these key phrases:

- Personal experience
- Inspires them to look inwards
- Discover their passion and their true path

You're going to see that my Passion Statement from 2011 is reflected in the thank-you letter from 2015 almost word for word!

Considering I actually had nothing to do with the thank-you letter (you can see it's addressed to the training company rather than me), this boggled my mind!

I realised that I just kept on working hard at it, and eventually, it just manifested itself, because I was so clear and passionate about it.

Live a life that is full of Experiences of sports, entertainment
Activities & Nature in a way that inspires others. To go
beyond their limits (set by others) and who be who
they truely want to be

I will do this through building a company that
provides these services which I will
Refine & develop its operation till its effecienctly
Run & profitabley Turning over sufficient amount
Of money To Make me Finnaly free to Enjoy and
provide a great support system to those who are
Involved in making it happen

THE ARAB EVANGELICAL EPISCOPAL CHURCH

المدرسة الأهلية للبنات
THE AHLIYYAH SCHOOL FOR GIRLS

تأسست ١٩٢٦
FOUNDED 1926

Ref: ASGBSA/30/4/2015

1st April, 2015

To: Mr. Khalid Qawwar
General Manager
TANWEER Business Consultancy & Training

Dear Mr. Qawwar,

On behalf of the Ahliyyah School for Girls and the Bishop's School for Boys, I
wish to express my gratitude for Dr. Hamawi's visit to our school last Saturday.
Dr. Mustafa Hamwi is an interesting man with an inspirational story to share.
Through sharing his personal experience with his audience and divulging details of
past contradictions and struggles, he inspires others to look inwards in order to
discover their passion and their true path. Humble, energetic, warm and passionate
Dr. Hamwi captures his audience with his honesty and presence. He uses his
personal journey in order to allow others to positively and critically reflect and
question their being and its meaning.

I recommend his workshop to anyone who wishes to take a moment out of their
busy lives to ponder, to realign, or simply to connect with someone who has found
his path and is happy to share.

Sincerely yours,

Senator Haifa Najjar
Superintendent
The Ahliyyah School for Girls
The Bishop's School for Boys

المملكة الأردنية الهاشمية ـ عمان / جبل عمان ـ هاتف: ٤٦٢٤٨٧٢ (٦ ٩٦٢) ـ فاكس: ٤٦٢١٥٤٩ (٦ ٩٦٢) ـ صندوق بريد: ٢٠٣٥ عمان ١١١٨١ الأردن
The Hashemite Kingdom of Jordan - Amman / Jabal Amman -Tel. (962 6) 4624872 Fax. (962 6) 4621549 - P.O. Box: 2035 Amman 11181 Jordan
E-mail: asg@asg.edu.jo   www.asg.edu.jo

THIS is where I get goose-bumps while I'm reading the story. I'm usually at a loss of words each time I even think of how this turned out. When I wrote this in 2011, I didn't even think this was going to be possible. This is *how* difficult it was when I wrote it, because I believed there was no way this was going to happen for me.

In less than five years (remember I asked you to think of your passionate life in a time frame of three to five years too!), my Passion Statement came true!

This is why the exercise I'm going to do with you next is critical. You need to be present, engaged, and inspired in every single way when you are writing this.

Start by doing a quick "Who are you in abundance?" meditation, as shown below.

Just keep repeating the question and then speak out the first intuitive answer that comes to mind. See the example below.

Who are you in abundance? I am joy.
Who are you in abundance? I am pain.
Who are you in abundance? I'm greed.
Who are you in abundance? I'm generosity.
Who are you in abundance? I am giving.
Who are you in abundance? I'm powerful.

When you think about abundance, it does not have to make sense. Just the word abundance brings out a lot of what's inside you. Keep doing this as many times as needed, till you *feel* like you are overflowing with abundance and are able to see the possibilities of your passionate future.

NOW, you are ready to move to the most important element, which is the peak of the Live Passionately process—drafting your Passion Statement.

The Passion Statement in its current form is an evolution of the first statement I wrote—an evolution that took many years. The more I used that statement, the more I started figuring out the best structure that can help people to write a comprehensive statement with ease.

I .... hereby declare before myself, others, and the universe that my primary passion and purpose in life is...

"I am the ...."

(You remember the money, power, or fame exercise? Which one were you? Were you the richest, the most powerful, or the most famous? Let's say your driving force is fame. Then you would say, "I am the most famous." If it's riches, then you would say, "I am the richest." How would you describe yourself in one word?)

The way I wrote mine in the early stages was "I am the most popular inspiration-through-passion speaker author and coach." So, this is how I explained myself at that time. Then that evolved into becoming, "I am the most inspirational Passionpreneur."

It's okay for you to write whatever comes to your mind. Remember, my first sheet was very scribbly with an ugly handwriting. Just write.

I have a life that is full of

....

....

....
....
....
....
....

Write a list of your top values—the things that you came up with on the Mind Map and the Time Distribution Sheet. In my case, it will be, "*I have a life that is full of nature, personal growth and learning, health and wellness, and adventure travel.*"

I am doing this through (a business/organisation/working in...) (Explain how you will do it.)

....
....
....
....
....
....
....

Who would you like to serve? Remember, "Passion is consistently doing what you love, what you are good, at and what is **of value to the world**." Who would you like to serve in the process? Explain how you will do it. Will you set up a business? Or work for a big organisation? How will you use your talents?

That helps...

....
....
....

....
....
....
....

Describe the target audience that you would you like to help. For me, it's aspiring, passionate people who would like to discover and live their passion.

Do/be
(Describe how you will serve them.)

....
....
....
....
....
....
....

What will you help your target audience to do or be with the service? For example, I help aspiring, passionate people become Passionpreneurs. I help them discover their passion and turn it into a business that they can live off and enjoy their life with. What do you want to help people do or be through your service?

So that they...
(Describe the value/benefits of your service to them.)

....
....
....
....
....

....
....

Describe the value and the benefits of your service to these people. For example, what's the benefit of people becoming Passionpreneurs? This will help them make an impact on the world and enjoy giving while they are making a great living and enjoying life every single day. This is the benefit. I want you to describe the benefits of your service in the same way.

And then, in the process of all of that, "I am..."
(Describe how are you changing the world through this process.)
....
....
....
....
....
....
....

You remember the last question I asked? What is the one thing (or two or three things) about the world that are irritating you and pissing you off that you would change if you had the resources? Well, guess what? Now it's time to put that in your Passion Statement.

I am enduring pleasure and pain on the journey of making it happen, and I'm loving every minute of it!

It is important for you to understand that you're going to endure pleasure and pain on the journey of making it happen. And you better love every minute of it!

Now that you've written your Passion Statement, I want you to date it. When? Not today. If you remember, three to five years from now. It will happen in that time frame, guaranteed. Do not rush and think, "I want to make it in a year," and do not push it beyond five years. You can write any date, but I want you to be specific about the *exact* date, month, and year.

Signed:
Date: / /20
(Date it three to five years from today's date.)

By the way, you're going to write your Passion Statement many times. I have re written mine 50, 60, 70 times. It's never going to be "perfect" because, on the journey of living a passionate life, you will gain more clarity on a daily basis, and your aspirations will grow with you.

My Passion Statement

I .... hereby declare before myself,
others, and the universe that my primary passion and purpose in life is that:

I am the (Richest, Most Powerful, Most Famous)

I have a life that is full of (list your top values.)

I'm doing this through (explain how you will do it and who do you serve in the process as per below)
a business/organisation that is helping (describe the target audience.)

- -

Do/be (Describe how you will serve them.)

So they (Describe the value/benefits of your service to them.)

And in the process of all of that I'm (Describe how are you changing the world through this process.)

I am enduring pleasure and pain on the journey of making
it happen, and I'm loving every minute of it!

Signed: ....

Date: ..../.............../............... (3–5 years from today's date)

Passion

Does your **Passion Statement cover?**

 All your top values

 Career and Work

 Spiritual

 Mental Development

 Social Life

 Financial

 Family and Relationships

 Physical and Health

Recreation and Fun

 Finally, does it put a big smile on your face or bring tears in your eyes when you think about it?

Quality Check

To make sure your Passion Statement is solid, make sure it covers:

- all your top values (if they are not covered, then go back and add them),
- spiritual success,
- career and work,
- finances,
- mental development,
- physical health,
- family and relationships,
- social life, and
- recreation and fun.

Finally, does it put a big smile on your face or bring tears to your eyes when you think about it? This is the litmus test. Because, if, after all of this, you're not jumping for joy, not moved to tears, not a bit scared, and not going, "Oh my god, this is so big. How can I do it?" then, my fellow Passionpreneur, you have not done this right.

Take time, put on some music, drink water, move around, come back, sit and work with it. This *is* something that's going to change your life, so please treat it as critical to a transformed life. Because if there's one thing it will do, it will change your life.

Passion Sketch

You might underestimate the value of this exercise due to its simplicity (and the fact that your drawing skills are as bad as mine ☺). However, there is a more exact science to this exercise than meets the eye.

I learned this exercise from my dear friend, Allan Pease, the father of body language. When you use a pen, you fire a hundred times more neurons in your brain than when you do not. Why? Because a picture has a different impact on your brain than words.

The picture and the sketch might look ugly, but your mind knows what you are trying to convey. Hey, look at the works of many great artists. You may scratch your head trying to understand something that the artist may speak for hours about!

So, I want you to sketch your Passionate Life based on the Passion Statement. The sketch could be as funny, as ugly, as beautiful, as stark, as complex or as simple as possible. It could be composed of stick figures; it could be random sketches; it could be scribbles. It does not matter because your mind sees what it wants to see: a *perfectly passionate future.*

If you can literally see yourself speaking to people, just draw a stick figure on a stage with lots of round heads and people saying, "Yay," "Wow," and so on. That's good enough; *that's* a Passion Statement manifested in a sketch. **The more time you spend sketching, the more it gets imprinted in your brain.**

My Passion Sketch

My Ideal Day

Now you've got the big picture, which is great. Can we bring it down to the specifics of how you would like to live your life day by day? There are two sides here. There's an ideal *day* design and there's an ideal *weekend* design.

Let's start with the **ideal day.** This is your working day. On the ideal day design sheet, which is what does your ideal working day look like, all you've got to do is assume you start your day at 6 and finish by 12 midnight. Even if you started at 5 and finished by 11, that's OK because this sheet is just a guideline.

Think of what would you like to do hour by hour. What would you like to do in every single hour, from the minute you open your eyes to the minute you close your eyes?

Now please, when you finish, go back and check: Does this design of an ideal day help you live your Passion Statement?

Does it align with all your values? Because if not, I promise you, something is wrong here. So they all have to align. Now let me be clear. I'm not asking you about your day design today. I'm not asking you about your day design next year.

I'm asking you about your ideal day design in three to five years' time. So please do not limit yourself in terms of dreaming about what you can achieve with an ideal day design.

I would like you to design an ideal weekend, which is as important as an ideal working day design. Remember that you want to be having fun. I work a lot, but I also like to have my fun, and I know exactly what fun means for me. I would like *you* to know what fun means for you.

So go ahead, and design your weekend. What time do you want to wake up? What are you going to do when you wake up, from the minute you wake up till the minute you sleep? Because when your weekend is as rich and as full and as fulfilling as your weekday, you're going to come back with a lot of energy and a lot of vigour to be passionate and have an impact on the world.

Now go on; design your ideal day and weekend.

What does your ideal WORKDAY look like?

5:00 am to 6:00 am	
6:00 am to 7:00 am	
7:00 am to 8:00 am	
8:00 am to 9:00 am	
9:00 am to 10:00 am	
10:00 am to 11:00 am	
11:00 am to 12:00 pm	
12:00 pm to 1:00 pm	
1:00 pm to 2:00 pm	
2:00 pm to 3:00 pm	
3:00 pm to 4:00 pm	
4:00 pm to 5:00 pm	
5:00 pm to 6:00 pm	
6:00 pm to 7:00 pm	
7:00 pm to 8:00 pm	
8:00 pm to 9:00 pm	
9:00 pm to 10:00 pm	
10:00 pm to 11:00 pm	
11:00 pm to 12:00 am	

What does your ideal WEEKEND look like?

5:00 am to 6:00 am	
6:00 am to 7:00 am	
7:00 am to 8:00 am	
8:00 am to 9:00 am	
9:00 am to 10:00 am	
10:00 am to 11:00 am	
11:00 am to 12:00 pm	
12:00 pm to 1:00 pm	
1:00 pm to 2:00 pm	
2:00 pm to 3:00 pm	
3:00 pm to 4:00 pm	
4:00 pm to 5:00 pm	
5:00 pm to 6:00 pm	
6:00 pm to 7:00 pm	
7:00 pm to 8:00 pm	
8:00 pm to 9:00 pm	
9:00 pm to 10:00 pm	
10:00 pm to 11:00 pm	
11:00 pm to 12:00 am	

Time to Reward Yourself, Well Done!

#LivePassionately

CHAPTER 7

VISUALISE YOUR PASSIONATE FUTURE

Passion Meditation

Imagination is more important than knowledge.

—Albert Einstein

See Your Passionate Future Today!

In this chapter, I'm going to help you understand the science behind visualisation and meditation and why this stuff works. We are going to do a creative visualisation to help you envision and see your passionate life NOW.

We're going to customise a meditation for you. Yes, your own Passion Meditation! So hold on. There is also a little gift for you since you made it so far—a Passion Meditation that you can download!

Why Meditation?

Before you start groaning that you can't meditate to save your life, read on to understand why I'm speaking about meditation.

Meditation can change the way your brain is wired. This is scientific, by the way. This is not hoo-ha talk. It can literally rewire your brain. This has been proven through years and years and years of study. Regardless of whether or not you believe in meditation, it's called the "mindfulness technique," which is a more scientific term, if that appeals to you.

The best way to imagine things is through visualisation and meditation; by doing these, you put yourself in a state where you're able to see images or words; you have a certain knowing or feeling about what you want out of life.

When you become clear about what you want, your mind will search for circumstances that will create it. Now you might have heard about *The Secret*; you might have heard about the Law of Attraction. All of this can be simply explained in scientific terms. Consider the *reticular activator* in the mind; this is a part of your mind that notices things using your peripheral vision, not your direct sight.

I'll give you an example. When you are single, you hardly notice babies in the mall. But as soon as you are expecting a baby, you walk into the mall—into the same exact mall that you've been to a hundred times before—and all you see are kids and babies and prams. You walk into the same mall where you used to see shops to buy your own clothes, and instead, you start noticing baby shops. How come? This is all due to the *reticular activator.*

Why does this happen? Is it because they were never there and they just appeared? No, they've always been there, but your mind was filtering them out because they were not necessary or import-ant for you. The minute you decide these things are important for you, your mind is going to find ways to make them present around you. This is exactly what the Law of Attraction is.

What does that have to do with meditation, you ask.

If you look up brain scans of people's brains before and after meditation, you will see that, before meditation, the brain is over-heating with a lot of red spots (heat is not very good for the brain), and within just 10 minutes of meditation, the red is replaced with blue and green colours, indicating calmness, showing you that the impact of the meditation is strong.

If you still don't believe me, check out this story:

During the late '60s, US Air Force Colonel George Hall was a pilot who was shot down over Vietnam and captured as a prisoner of war where he spent 7.5 years in a POW concentration camp. Later, in 1973, he went to play golf. That's about 13 years later after his capture and about 6 years from his release. He went on to play in a pro-am competition, and he got high scores in that game. I'm not a big golfer, so I can't tell you what the handicap means, but the actual number that he scored is 76. If you're a golfer, you know what that means; all I know is that this is very high in the game of golf.

How did he do that when he never actually played golf all those years when he was in prison?

He says he spent those years practising in his mind. He was visualising every single shot, every single move, every single muscle, every single movement of his body—of his arms, his ankles, and his twist—and guess what? That's what helped him win this competition. Now, this is not my answer, and this is not a story. You can look it up on the internet, and you will find it. Also, this is not the only story in the world that tells you about people who have achieved amazing things by imagining and visualising them.

Now, please do not get me wrong. I don't want to get caught up in this whole Law of Attraction and the *Secret* stories where you think that by sitting and imagining a million dollars they're going to appear. Because you're still going to have to go out and make things happen.

However, this process is going to help you rewire your brain to be more receptive to the opportunities of living a Passionate Life when they present themselves to you. Remember, we are attempting to take out all of the old negative histories and memories from you, and we are replacing them now with a new visualisation of how the future is going to be, so it looks real.

The Passion Meditation
To help you on your Live Passionately journey, we have produced a special customised passion meditation that is only available for the Passion Community.

Go to http://www.moustafa.com/PassionTools and enter the code 7,777,777 to download your bonus pack which includes the passion meditation, an inspirational posters deck, a guide to turning your passion into a successful business, and access to the Passion Tribe private Facebook Group.

For you to get the best out of the meditation, let's create a customised version for you. Please refer to the "Visualisation Process Sheet" here.

Commit to meditating at least once a week. That's only a 15-minute meditation in a week of 9,900 minutes. If you do not have enough passion for that, then maybe you are not serious about living a passionate life, or you are just being lazy!

I do 15–30 minutes of mediation daily; sometimes I go up to 45 minutes in a single day. If you want your passionate life to manifest, you're going to have to do this.

How to customise your Passion Meditation.

"I set the time on my calendar, for every..."
(Define the hour and day.)

Now please run through this process with me. First, take a deep breath.

Pull out your Passion Statement. Look at it, and take a deep breath. Visualise where are you going to be in three to five years when you have achieved the goals on your Passion Statement.

I am at...
(Where are you? What is the place? How would you describe it?)

I see...
(What do you see? What things, people, or other living beings do you see?)

I hear...
(What sounds do you hear when you're living your Passionate Life?)

I smell...
(What kind of fragrances or aromas feed your senses?)

I taste...
(What do you taste in your mouth?)

I feel...
(What do you feel? What overwhelming passion, joy, happiness, or fulfilment do you experience?)

Creative Visualisation
Process

 I set time on my calendar every ....
at .... to visualise

I am at .... I smell ....

I see .... I taste ....

I hear .... I feel ....

Whatever the mind can conceive and believe, it can achieve.

—Napoleon Hill

Now that you've written your customised Passion Visualisation script, you can use the Passion Meditation audio we have specially produced for you.

When you reach the audio via the link shared, please turn your phone on flight mode, and make sure you will not be disturbed for those 15 minutes. Put your headset on, and follow the instructions on this meditation; use whatever you've written on the script to help you visualise that.

Time to Reward Yourself, Well Done!

#LivePassionately

CHAPTER 8

BUILD YOUR PASSION TRIBE

You Cannot Have a Party on Your Own

If you want to go fast, go alone. If you want to go far, go together.

—African Proverb

Let's Make Things More Fun
In this chapter, we're going to talk about your Passion Tribe—what it is and why you need one.

Then we're going to talk about the kind of people you want in your Passion Tribe and the kind of people you should avoid when you're on a journey of living passionately. You're then going to take steps to start your own Passion Tribe.

Before we start, please take a step back, and reflect on your Passion Statement.

Review your Passion Statement. Are there any changes or updates to it? If there are, please make the changes, and rewrite your Passion Statement. I hope there are, actually, because as you're progressing and moving forwards, you are most likely going to have more thoughts and more clarity. Therefore, your Passion Statement will evolve even at this point!

What Is a Passion Tribe?
On the journey of being passionate, going alone is going to get very hard. I've learned this the hard way. When I started my journey of being a speaker, author, and coach, my dear God, it was harder than I could have thought of in my worst nightmare! And coming back from what was initially a one-way ticket from India, imagine how hard it was for me to hang out with people who I was

now certain were more energy vampires than people that were actually helping me.

They were dragging me down; they were telling me to anything I would say or put forth. I would say something, and they would shoot back the same thing, either verbally or in their facial expressions or with their body language. They always seemed to be saying, "WHAT are you talking about?"

Beware! It is people like these who are going to drag you down and hold you back.

And this is why you need to have a group of passionate people that is going to support you, rather than hold you back, as you progress full throttle towards living a passionate life. It is *these* people whom I define as a Passion Tribe. *These* are the people that you have to CONSCIOUSLY surround yourself with. They're not going to just suddenly appear around you, and if you're making a transformation in your life, it's not going to be with the same group of people!

For this Passion Tribe to be built, you have to know two things: there's a group of people that you want and a group of people that you **do not** want on that Passion Tribe.

Who Should Be in Your Passion Tribe?

Let's start with the kinds of people that you do want on your Passion Tribe.

1. People who **SHARE THE SAME VALUES**
    What does that mean? If, through this exercise, you have found that one of your values is personal growth, then people who share the same value would be people who

love personal growth. If you value nature and travel, then people who share the same values would be the kind of people you want on your Passion Tribe.

So why do you need these kinds of people? Well, simply because it's an automatic match when you share the same values. This means they will understand you better. They will feel what you are feeling. They will know what you want to talk about before you even start talking about it, as opposed to somebody you're talking to who does not share that value.

2. People who are **ON A SIMILAR JOURNEY**

These are people who might not necessarily share the same values. However, they are taking the same steps towards the kind of life that you want to live. Let's say you have the value of personal growth and you are on an entrepreneurial journey that involves launching your restaurant business.

And maybe there's another person who does not value personal growth, maybe does not even value food, but is on a journey of opening a restaurant business or has been successful in the restaurant business. This is the kind of person you want in your Passion Tribe. Because although you might not share the same values, you are on a journey of building a business, and *that's* a common factor between you two.

You can compare notes, you can talk about what you have learnt, you can talk about what works and what doesn't work, and you can share resources, so that's an important kind of person to have in your Passion Tribe.

3. People who share the **SAME INTERESTS AND ASPIRATIONS**

What does this mean? These people might not have the same values. They might not even be on the journey of pursuing a passionate life; however, they have an interest in things that you like. Having these people as a part of your Passion Tribe is going to give you a type of support group that you can talk to about anything.

Maybe they're interested in food and you are too. Maybe they don't place a high value on personal growth; maybe they don't want to develop so much. Maybe they don't want to open a restaurant business, but they're big foodies who like to hang around at restaurants and talk about food.

Guess what? *These* are people that will make you feel good while you're on the journey. You *are* going to learn a lot from them.

The big question is this: "Where do you find them?"

Think about fan pages and fan groups; think about online groups; think about meetups. Go online and search. Start on the Passion Community Facebook page that you're a part of; I'm sure you're going to find people who share some of your interests.

Now if you go and do all of this and you still do not find people with the same interests, guess what? You are probably going to be the first person and the leader/ owner who's going to do this by yourself.

Do you think that when I started, there were groups of Passionpreneurs cheering me up? I *started* the group. So why not you? Become the leader of whatever you are seeking. So if I'm the passion guy, you go be the food guy or the food girl. You be whatever you want to be as long as you're truly passionate about it.

4. **PROFESSIONALS**

These are people like coaches, speakers, authors, and mentors. Now why do you need these people in your Passion Tribe? They are different from the other three kinds; these are people who have the right resources. They have the right tools, tips, and techniques to be able to help you without being dragged into your story. Why is that?

a. They have **no emotional attachment**. If you come to me and I'm coaching you, I'm not on your emotional journey. Therefore, if you're feeling up or down, it does not impact me. I'm looking at this the same way a doctor looks at the patient and helps the patient. There's no emotional journey; if *you* are feeling down, they're not going to get dragged down with you. Things are different with the other kinds of people whom you might have some personal relation or shared interest with. If the economy is down, all of you might end up feeling depressed. *But a professional is simply looking at everything with objectivity.*

b. They have **a fresh perspective**. You might see the other groups more regularly or connect with them more regularly, but a professional is somebody you see at a certain pace. So if you're going to talk to a coach once every two weeks or once a month, guess what? That person is looking at it from a fresh, outside perspective, since they are not engaged in all the drama that you've been having to go through for a few weeks.

c. They **have the tools**. They're not guessing. The other groups of people are still in the process of trial and error; they're talking from their experiences, which might or might not fit you or be right for you.

d. A professional is **following scientific processes**. They follow process steps; they follow tried-and-tested techniques, and they have done this for hundreds and thousands of people. They have spent

BUILD YOUR PASSION TRIBE

thousands and thousands of hours on the topic that you're trying to get help on.

So guess who's going to be able to help you more?

That being said, you need all four kinds of people. It's not an either/or situation. You need each of them because each of them is going to come at things from a unique angle; only then can you have a proper Passion Tribe. You need at least one of each of those kinds of people in your tribe available for you.

People You Definitely Want to AVOID

Who you *have* in the tribe is important, but *who you do NOT have and want* is equally important. So let's talk about the four kinds of people whom you **do not want** in your Passion Tribe.

1. **Naysayers**. These are the angry-Smurf type of people who, no matter what, are going to come to you and say no. Whatever you tell them elicits a, "No, it can't be done. It can't work." They're just eating up your energy and putting you down, no matter what you try to do.

2. **Haters.** Man, is the world full of haters?! I mean, did you do anything wrong to them? No. But do they hate you? Yes. Why? Simply because your success is a proof of their failures. Usually these people are lazy; they don't want to do anything, and they would hate to see anybody who's successful. Maybe they've tried once and failed. And if you try and succeed, it reminds them that they have failed. And they don't want to recognise that failure; they don't want to try harder, so they will put you down. RUN. Run away from them.

3. **Jealous people.** They are just jealous, and they hate for you to be successful. Maybe they don't want the success,

but they just don't want *you* to be successful. You know they say, "Misery loves company." So stay away from this kind.

4. **Fearful people.** They have a lot of fear, and they're projecting their fear on you. You know what's interesting? Usually, this can be found in the people closest to us. It could be family; it could be close and old-time friends.

Why? Simply because they love us. What happens is that because they love us so much and they might have been through a bad or a negative experience before, they project that fear on us and come and tell us, "No, don't do this. This doesn't work; that doesn't work."

They don't hate you, they have no negative intentions towards you, but they don't want to see you get hurt. Does that mean that what they're saying is right? Most probably not, because they speak from their own experience. As far as these people are concerned, just receive them with love. Don't get me wrong. I'm not asking you to get rid of your loved ones and your friends; all I'm asking you to do is compartmentalise the discussions you have with certain kinds of people.

With your loved ones, only share your successes. Don't share a lot of your challenges because that will make them scared for you. Share how things are working. Tell them about the things that you need for emotional support, but keep in mind that maybe they're not the best people to give you the emotional support you will need from time to time on your journey of living passionately.

What Do You Bring to the Table?

Not only is it important to ask this question to the other members of the Passion Tribe but it is also important to ask it to yourself.

You want to also be clear on what you bring to the table for a few reasons.

- A Passionate Life involves give and take.
- It will be much easier for you to convince people to help you, if you start by offering them value.
- Most people who are focused on goals will probably want to understand what value you add to their lives before they get close to you or allow you to get close to them.

Building your Passion Tribe is going to make this journey really, really fun, because you're going to feel empowered when you're surrounded by people as passionate as you are!

I hope you are taking action, and if you aren't, start *now*, **now**, NOW. Go on the Facebook group of the Passion Community and post, "I've just finished my Live Passionately programme, and I'm looking for people for my Passion Tribe."

Now that you thought about all angles of your Passion Tribe go ahead and fill in "My Passion Tribe" sheet, and do your best to include one of each of the suggested types.

Time to Reward Yourself, Well Done!

#LivePassionately

MY Passion Tribe

Name Person or Group	Kind Values/Journey/Intereststs	What they can do for me Guide/Support/Encourge	What do I bring to the table?

CHAPTER 9

AM I REALLY PASSIONATE NOW?

Whatever you are, be a good one.

—Abraham Lincoln

I cannot say this enough: WELL DONE!

If I were around you as you reached *this* stage of the journey, I would be jumping for joy. I hope you are! The level of excitement I usually have when someone starts the journey of a truly passionate life is off the charts. I'm already excited for you without even seeing you because I know this is the feeling I have when I achieve something that I'm passionate about. Actually, I hope you're **10** times more excited than me. I hope you're jumping with joy and screaming from the depths of your heart so that the whole world can hear you.

There's one more important little step for us to do. Remember what I promised you when you started this book? I promised you that you're going to get an increase in clarity and motivation when it comes to your passion in life.

So let's rewind to that sheet. Please go back to the Passion Clarity and Motivation sheet on page 29. On the third line it says, "How clearly do you know your passion?" I want you to answer that.

The second question is, "How excited are you about life overall?" Think about this. Did your excitement increase after all of this? I hope it did.

From years of doing this work, we usually get an average 20%–30% increase in clarity and motivation.

I found **my passion** and got **more clarity** or **further assurance** on what makes me **tick**

☐ **Yes**, and I am fulfilled

☐ **No**, the action step to make it a **YES** is ....

....

....

to be completed by ..../............../**20**............

And the last question I want to ask you is this: "Did you find your passion and get more clarity and further assurance on what you're doing?" Because, maybe after doing all of this, you just found out that you are already on the right track. So you either got more clarity or more assurance, maybe even both!

If the answer after all these steps is yes and you are fulfilled, then tick the box.

If, for some reason, the answer is no, then please write down the next action step you are going to take to make this a yes and put a deadline next to it. You know the game...

Passionate people do not wait for life to happen to them; they happen to life.

—*Moustafa Hamwi*

You need to know what's missing so you can take responsibility to close the gap. IF you still clearly haven't discovered your passion and you're not as motivated as you wanted to be, then what step are you going to take and when is it to be completed by?

And remember that you have made a commitment; you are going to live true to your passion that you have found through this book, and you are going to do what it takes to make this happen.

You have made this commitment, so please live up to it because there's nothing more that I wish than seeing you live in a fully passionate, fully engaged, and fully committed way.

PARTY LIKE A ROCK STAR

CELEBRATION TIME

PARTY TIME

Well, now you get more than just a small reward; you get a BIG reward for finishing the whole programme!

Time to make that celebration plan a reality.

Reach out to your Passion Tribe; announce it on social media; tell your friends, your family, and the WHOLE world that you are a step closer towards Living Passionately to manifest your greatness!

You think I am exaggerating and over the top? Remember the top level in being passionate is being enthusiastic and energetic; you shouldn't be afraid to show your level of energy.

Never forget:

> Passionate people do not wait for life to happen to them; they happen to life.
>
> —Moustafa Hamwi

So **go happen to life.** Build your legacy and let the story of your life be told. Let people say that you refused to live anything less than a life worth dying for!

Live Passionately
Moustafa Hamwi
The Passionpreneur

#LivePassionately

WANT MORE PASSION?

About This Book

DO YOU KNOW WHAT MAKES YOU TICK?

Without knowing the answer to this question, you will always feel like something is missing, no matter how successful you are. This is how Moustafa felt many years ago while he was running a multi million dollar business in Dubai and living a seemingly successful life.

THIS QUESTION TRIGGERED Moustafa TO START A JOURNEY— AN INNER SEARCH—OF TRUE PASSION, PURPOSE, AND MEANING, which eventually led him to buying a ONE-WAY TICKET TO INDIA IN 2012. Since his return in 2013, he invested all his time and effort into studying and researching the topic of passion and conducting in-person interviews with, to date, 160+ global leaders, authors, speakers, coaches, celebrities, Olympians, and Nobel prize laureates, diving deep into their interpretation of passion and its impact on all aspects of success in life and work.

All that he has learnt has been distilled into this book, which moves you from concepts and theories into integrated end-to-end processes, tools, and techniques. So if you are looking for an opportunity to bring passion back into your life in a way that will positively impact your career, business, relationships, and lifestyle like never before, then you are holding the right tool to do that.

If you are just itching to build the life you're dying to live, then this interactive book will help you *design a life truly worth living*. Through a simple and enjoyable process, it will help you to #LivePassionately.

About the Author

If you read the book, you will know who Moustafa is by now, but just in case you are flipping the pages before you buy the book, then here is a quick brief about him:

Moustafa is an award-winning author, speaker, and coach; he is recognised as the world's leading expert on passionate leadership.

In one year, he has achieved what took others 20 years to achieve in this industry. He was globally nicknamed the Passionpreneur due to his amazing success in empowering leaders to work and live passionately.

His philosophy is to live life so fully that it becomes a life worth dying for.

And, to be clear, to #LivePassionately means taking care of all angles of life, not only work. So he always recommends a healthy dose of adventure, nature, yoga, meditation, social work, and lots of network building on a global scale to create a Passion Tribe.

Go to www.Moustafa.com for more info on how to live passionately.

Speaking Opportunities

Interested in Injecting an Extra Dose of Passion at Your Event and Unleashing Passion, Leadership, and Innovation Within Your Organisation?

Moustafa delivers talks about using passion as a competitive advantage to dominate your market niche. He is the #1 choice if you're looking for a keynote speaker to talk about the use of passion to empower leadership, anticipate trends, and entice innovation.

Top Reasons Why Moustafa Is a Perfect Fit for Your Event

FOR THE AUDIENCE:
Moustafa's talks are described as "energetic, insightful, and engaging."

- **RELATABLE:**
  - Given his 19+ years of experience in a diversified portfolio of industries, he has worked with businesses, corporate executives, entrepreneurs, consultants, and

agencies. As a result, audiences will relate to Moustafa's substance and depth.

- **ENGAGING AND HIGH IMPACT:**
  - Moustafa's talks are energetic, insightful, and engaging. He will make every minute count. Members of your audience will be moved and inspired while gaining practical tools to improve their performance and quality of life.
- **REAL TAKEAWAY VALUE:**
  - Your audience will leave with lots of AHA! moments, meaningful tools, helpful frameworks, and techniques that can be immediately applied to real-world challenges.
- **CAPTIVATING STORIES:**
  - Concepts are delivered through rich storytelling, not boring professorial directives. Emotionally charged stories help the audience retain key points while enjoying a highly entertaining experience.

FOR THE EVENT ORGANISER:

Moustafa spent years running one of the largest and most successful event agencies in Dubai.

- **WE ARE ON YOUR SIDE:**
  - We know things could go wrong, but when Moustafa is on stage, he is able to manage the energy in the room and turn mishaps into opportunities to increase engagement.
- **NO DRAMA:**
  - We know what it means to put on a successful event, so we make your life easier. There will be no outrageous demands and no diva-like requests. Instead, Moustafa is professional, supportive, and resourceful.

- **WELL ORGANISED:**
  - Everything is considered from the angle of an event organiser first, so things are preplanned and well executed.
- **VISUALLY STUNNING PRESENTATIONS:**
  - Coming from a media industry background, Moustafa is very aesthetically driven. You won't see bullet point lists or text-heavy screens. Instead, audiences are dazzled with high-resolution photography, energising HD video clips, memorable props, and gorgeous visual transitions to add a flair to your event.

Bottom line—there's no business like show business; we love it!

For more info on booking Moustafa for a speaking engagement, get in touch with our Passion Assistant directly at pa@moustafa.com

Go Global

Want to Become a Global Thought Leader and a Celebrity Influencer?

You spent years becoming the best in your industry; NOW is the time to become a global **thought leader** and **celebrity influencer**.

We help you to get recognised as the "go-to" authority in your niche, to monetise your personal brand and to attract more of your ideal clients—that is, to DOMINATE YOUR MARKET.

If you are a
PROFESSIONAL EXPERT
(Executive, Entrepreneur, Coach, Speaker),
we help you
GET RECOGNISED AS A GLOBAL THOUGHT LEADER and
A CELEBRITY INFLUENCER
by helping you
find your niche, publish your book in three to six months, and
build your influencer site

OR,

if you are ALREADY AN AUTHORITY IN MY FIELD and have
a CONSIDERABLE FOLLOWING,
we help you
MONETISE YOUR BRAND
through
consulting and done-for-you services that create your product
offer, build your sales funnels, and help you pitch to your
audience from stage.

Get in touch directly with our Passion Assistant on
pa@moustafa.com for more info on how to become the
"go-to" authority in your niche.

Notes

Lightning Source UK Ltd.
Milton Keynes UK
UKHW012017150919
349837UK00001B/3/P